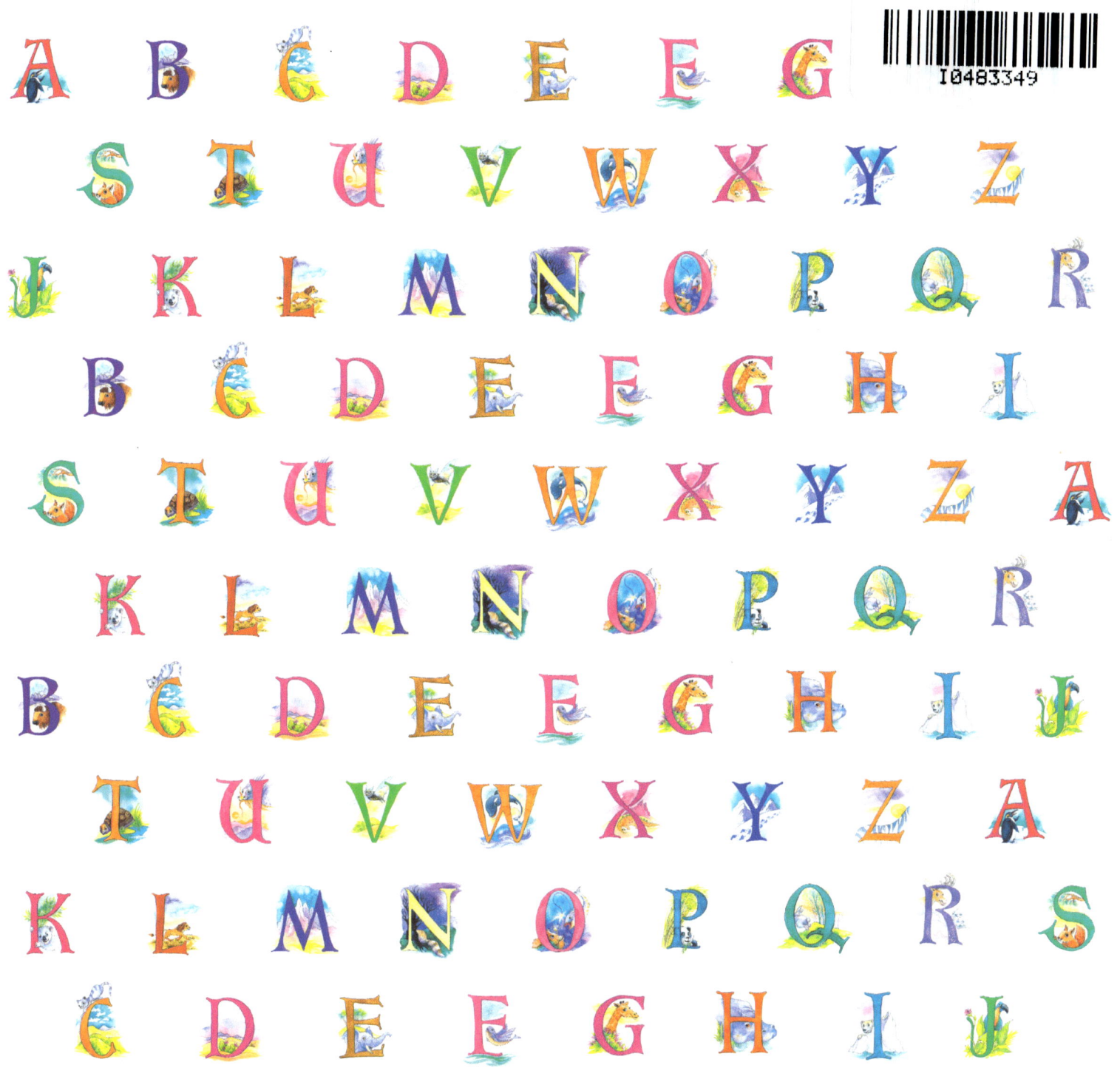

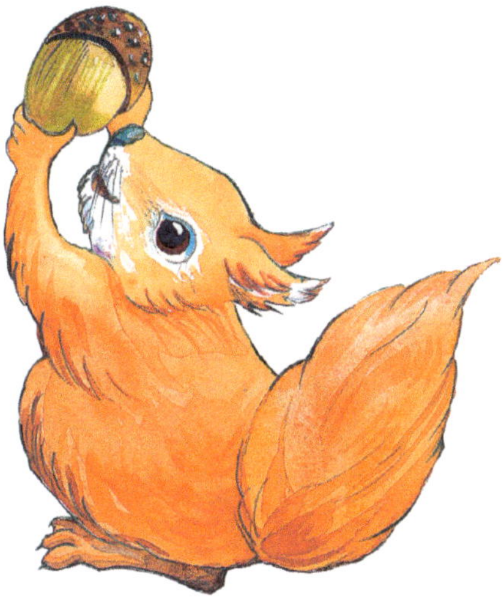

A B C D E E G H

Z

Y

X

W

V

I

J

K

L

M

Ex libris

Blessed is the one who reads . . .

REVELATION 1 : 3

U T S R Q P O N

For Catherine and Christopher
and all the children who love books

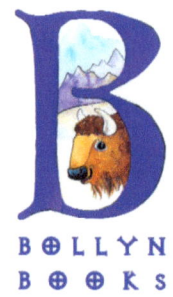

BOLLYN
BOOKS

Published in the United States
by Bollyn Books

First published as a Special Limited Edition 2006
This edition published 2013

www.bollynbooks.com

Library of Congress Control Number: 2013903446
ISBN 978-0-9853225-0-2

Printed in the U.S.A.

Christopher Bollyn & Helje Kaskel

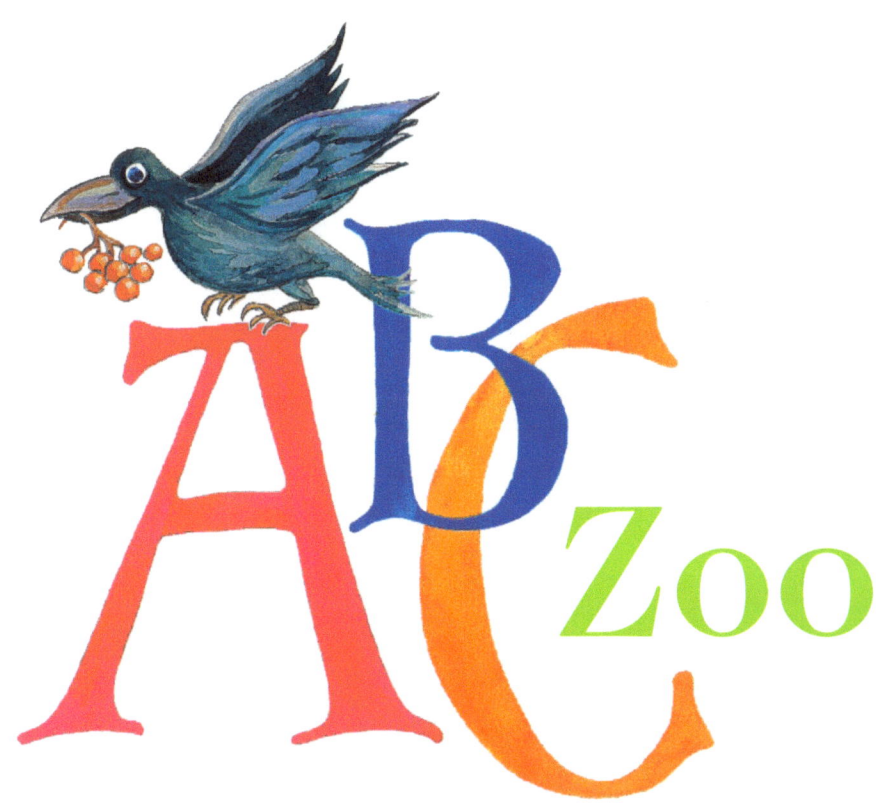

ABC Zoo

A celebration of art, decorated letters, and clever rhymes

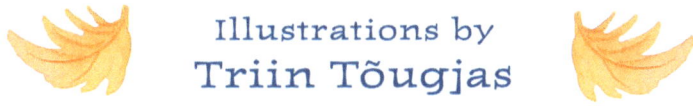

Illustrations by
Triin Tõugjas

A is for animals,

Some big and some small,

Read through this book

And discover them all.

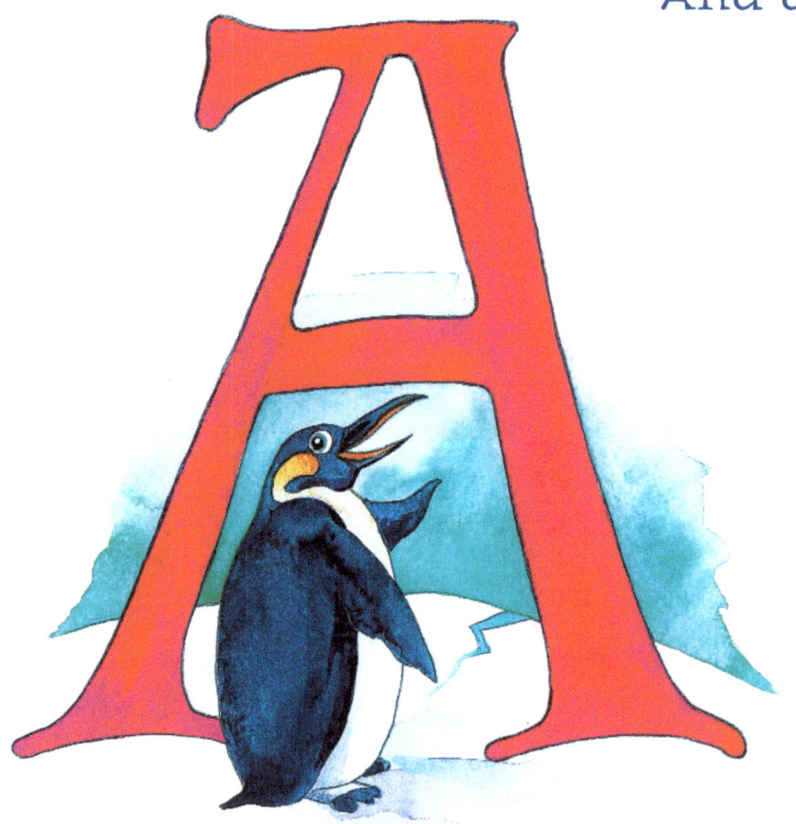

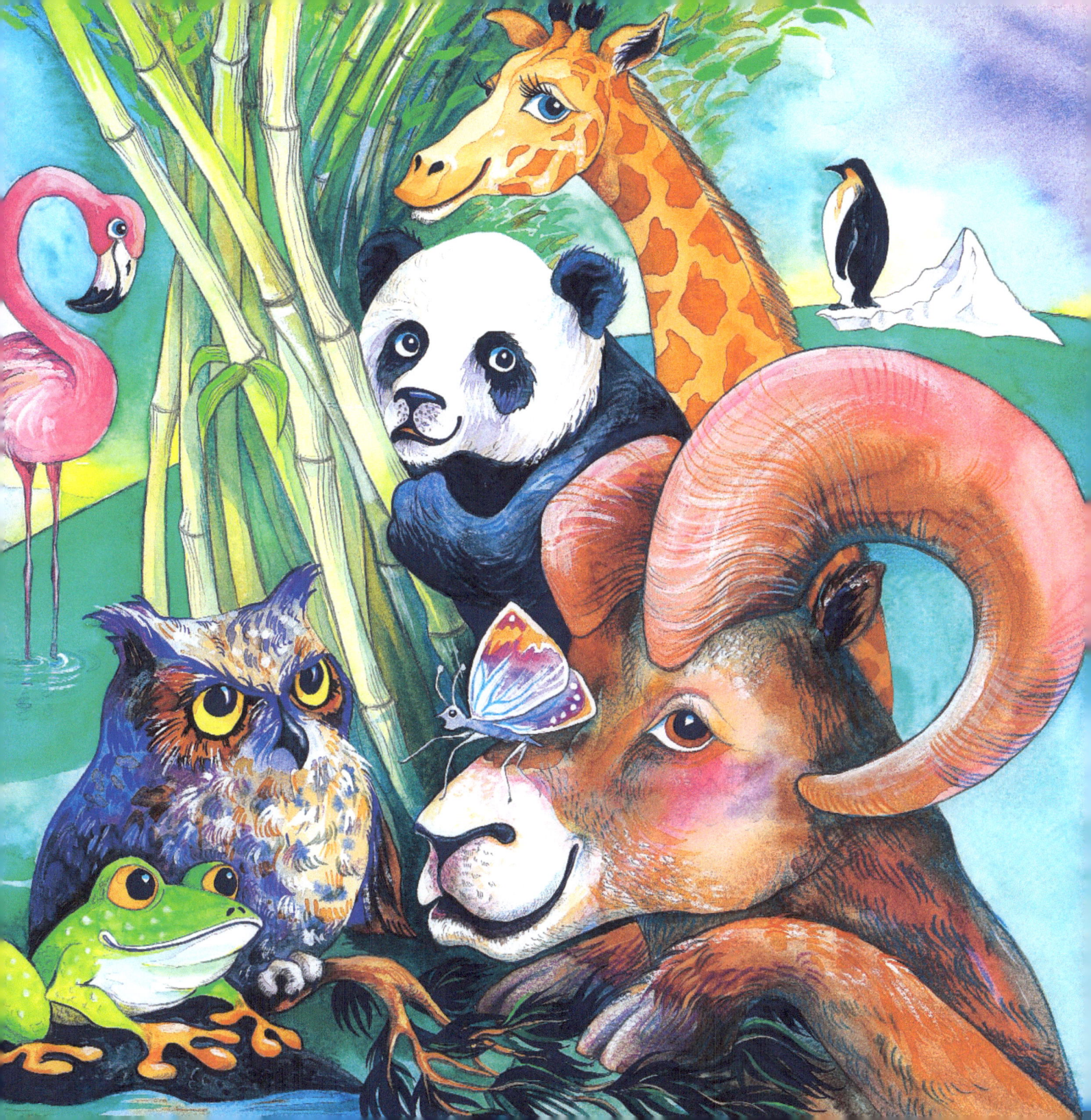

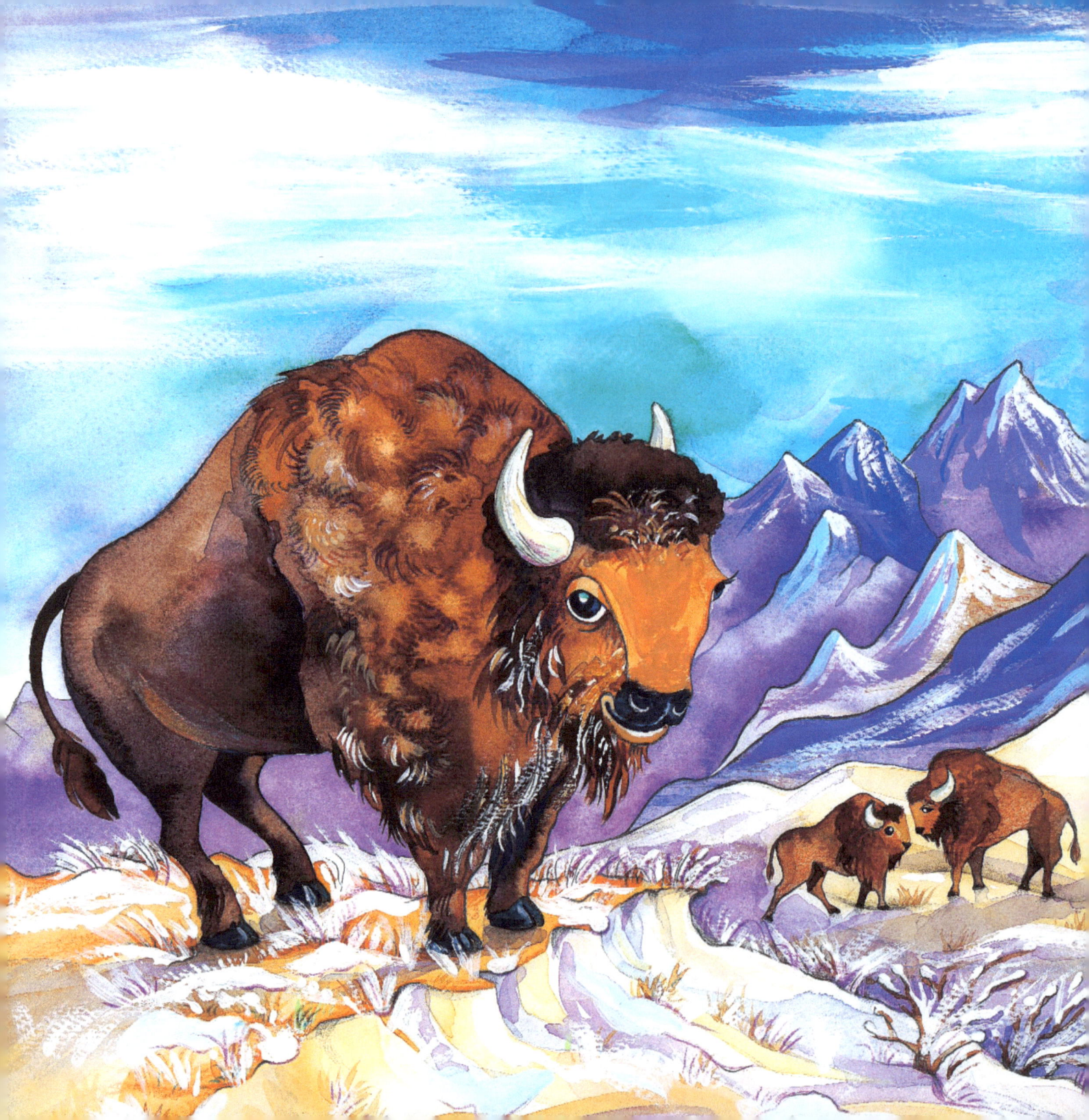

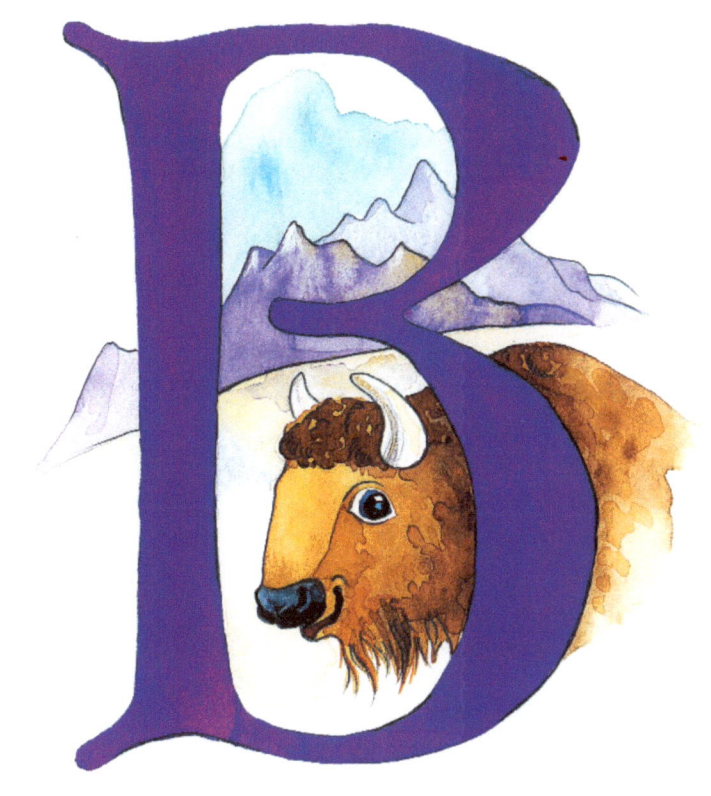

B is for bison

Roaming the plain,

Who keeps himself warm

With his long shaggy mane.

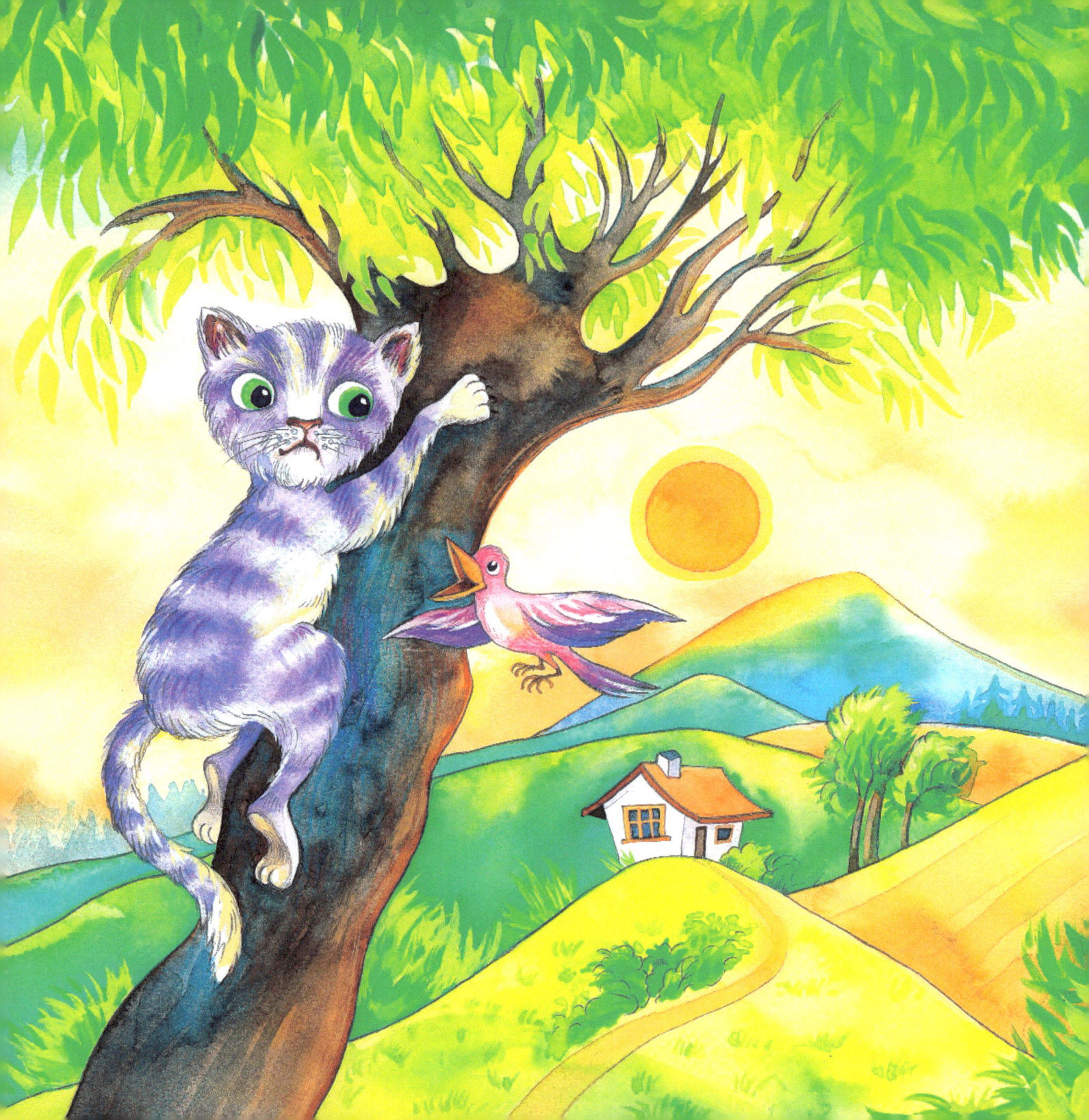

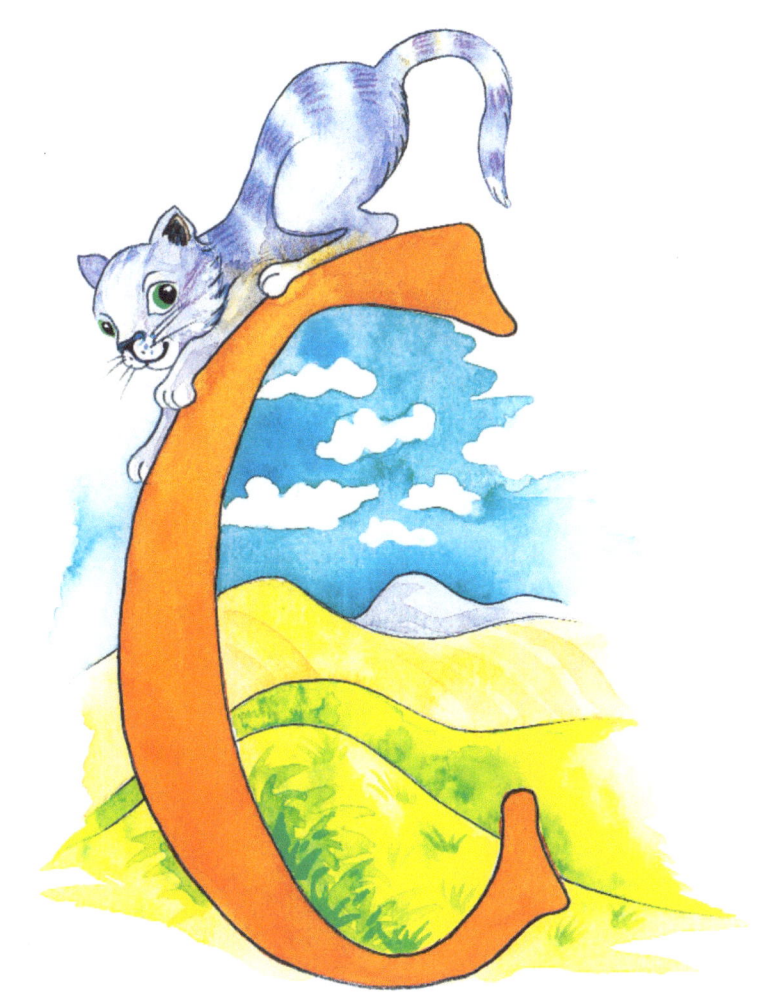

C is for cat
Caught in a tree,
She may stay there a while –
She'll just have to see.

D is for desert,

A hot and dry place,

Where in between cactus

Roadrunners race.

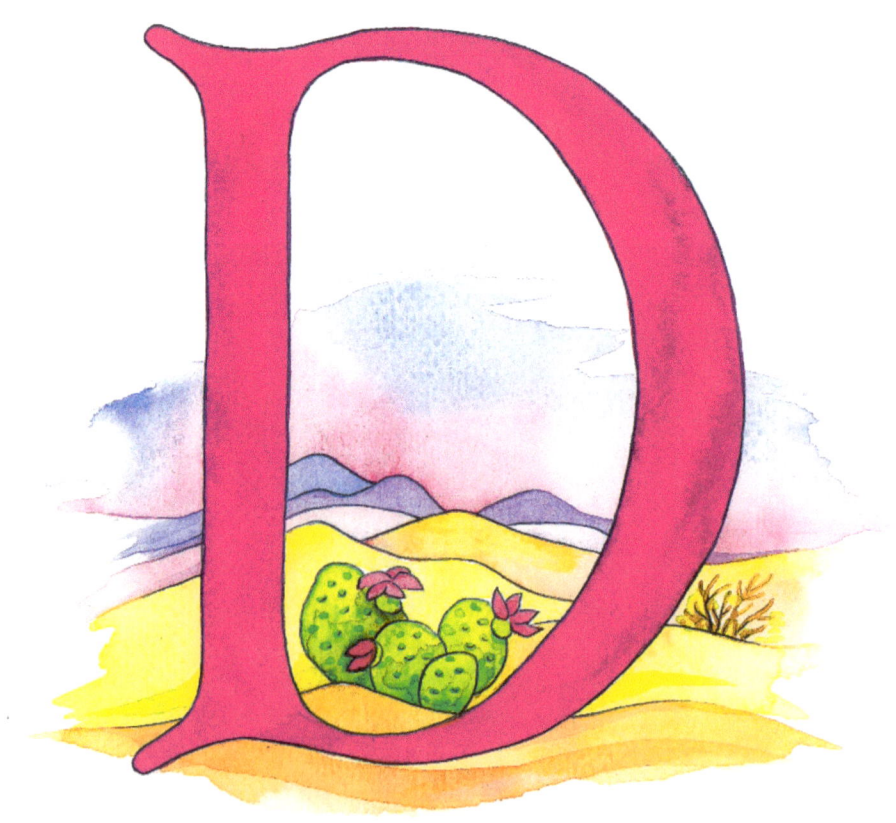

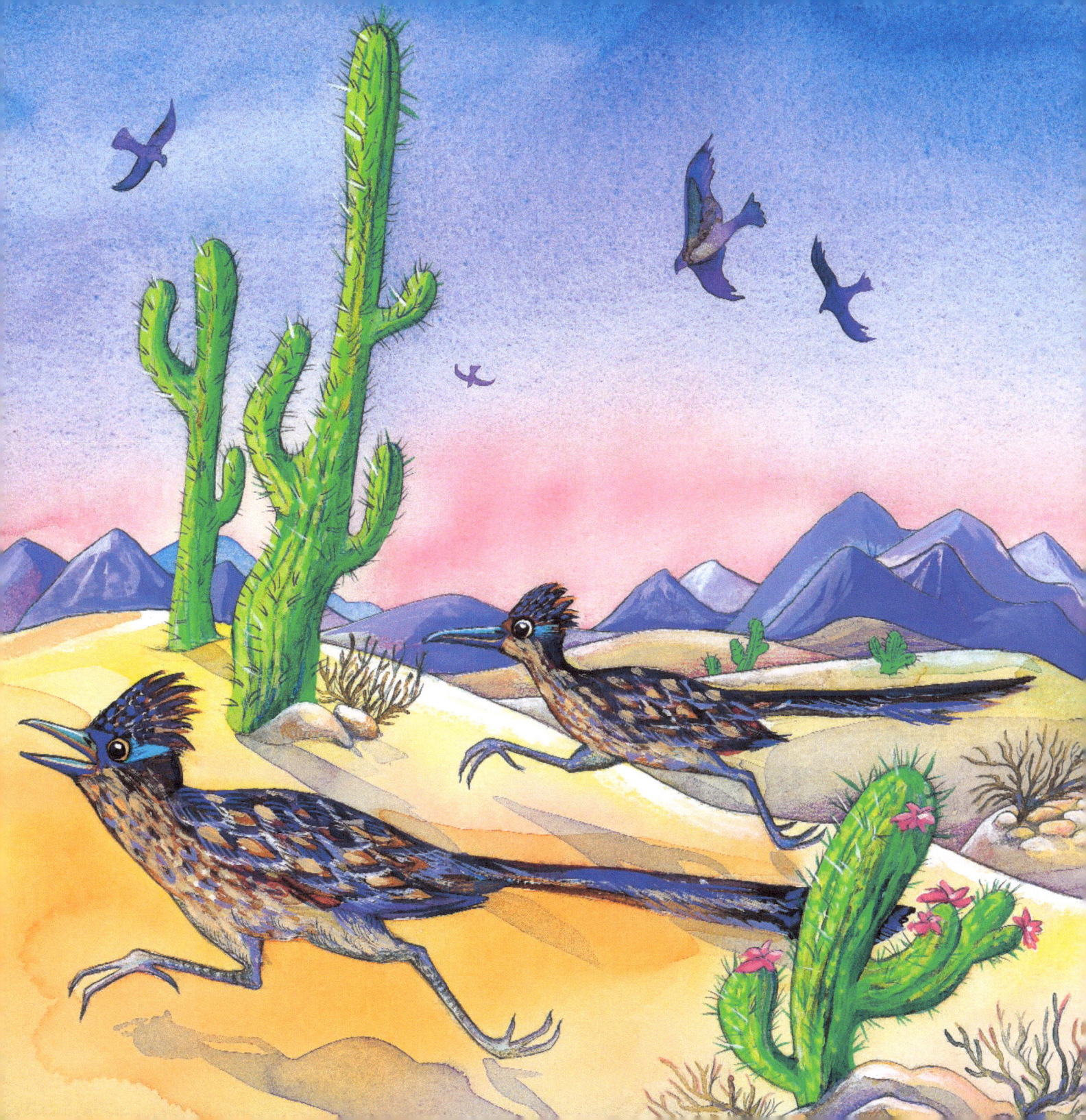

E is for elephant
As big as a house,
Listening to tales
Being told by a mouse.

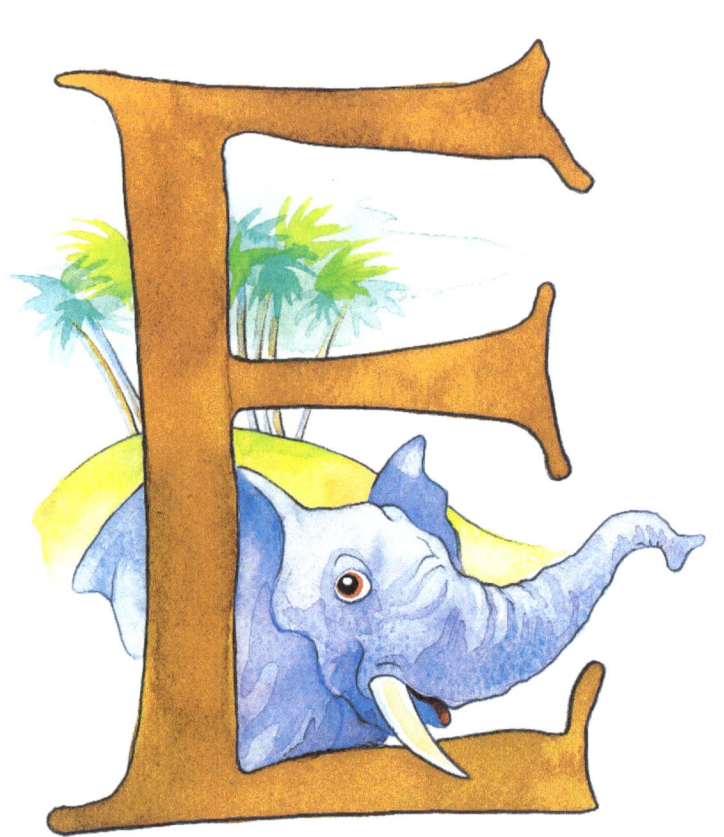

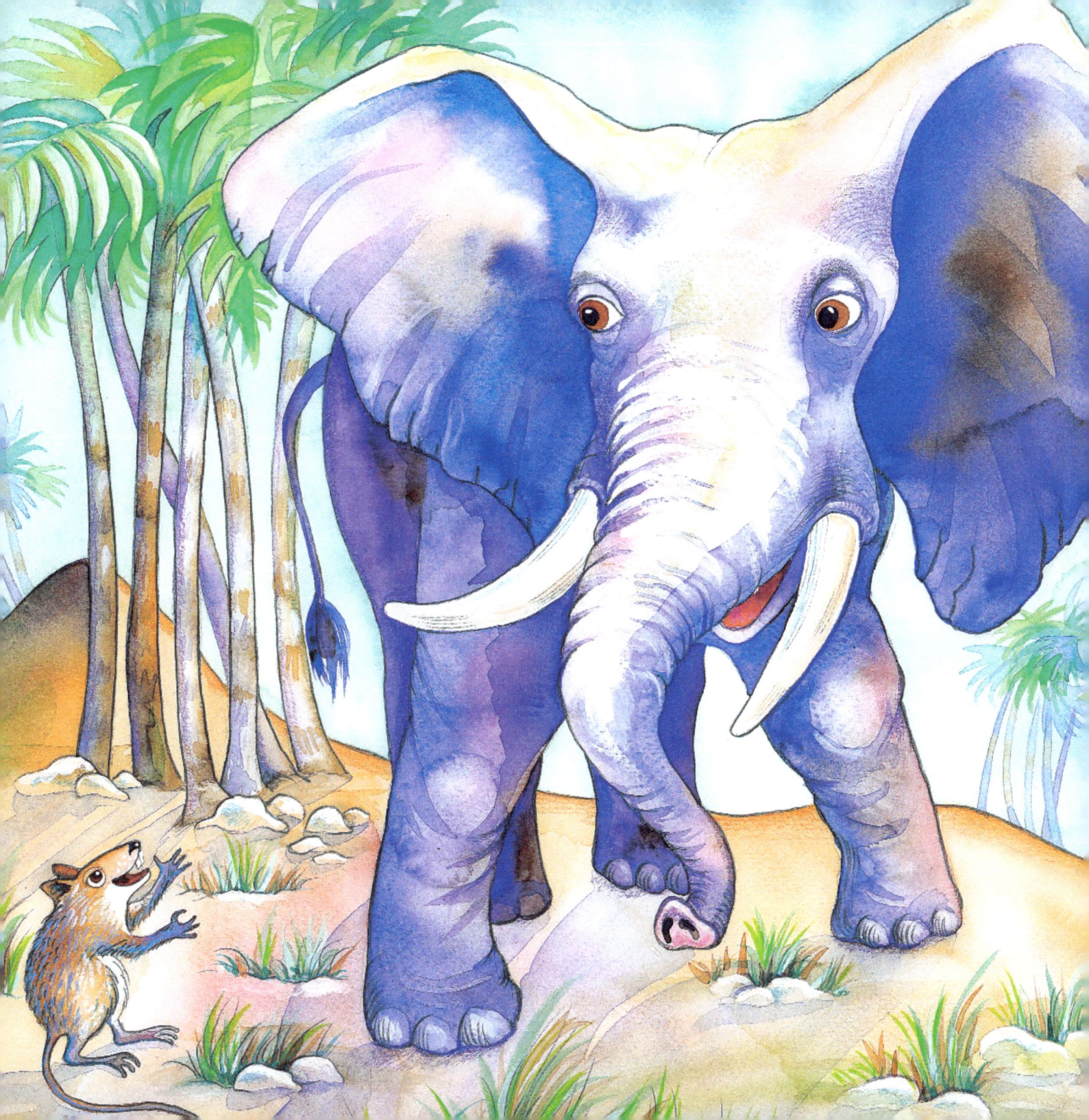

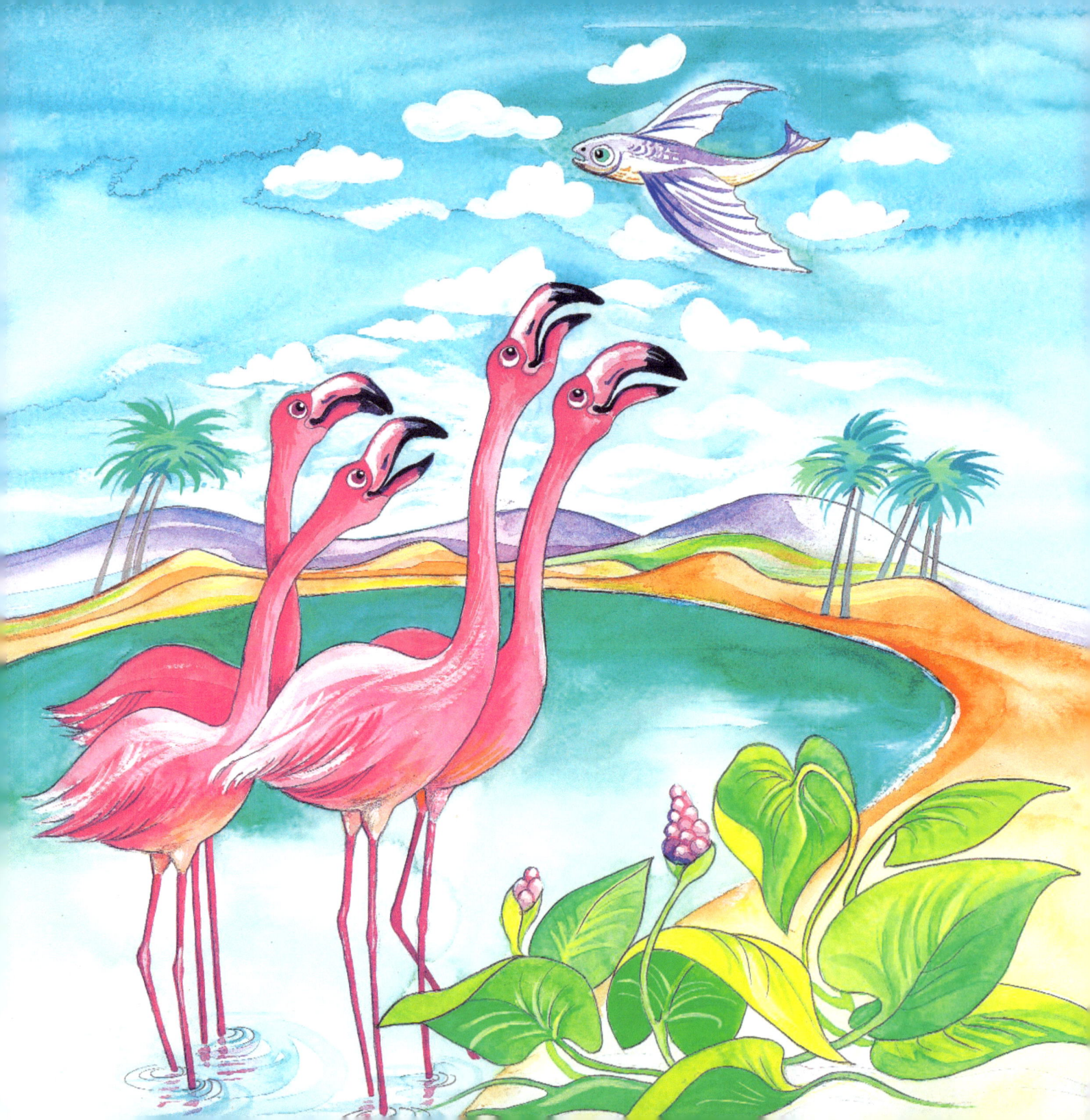

F is for fish

Flying high in the sky and

Flamingos who wonder,

"What's that going by?"

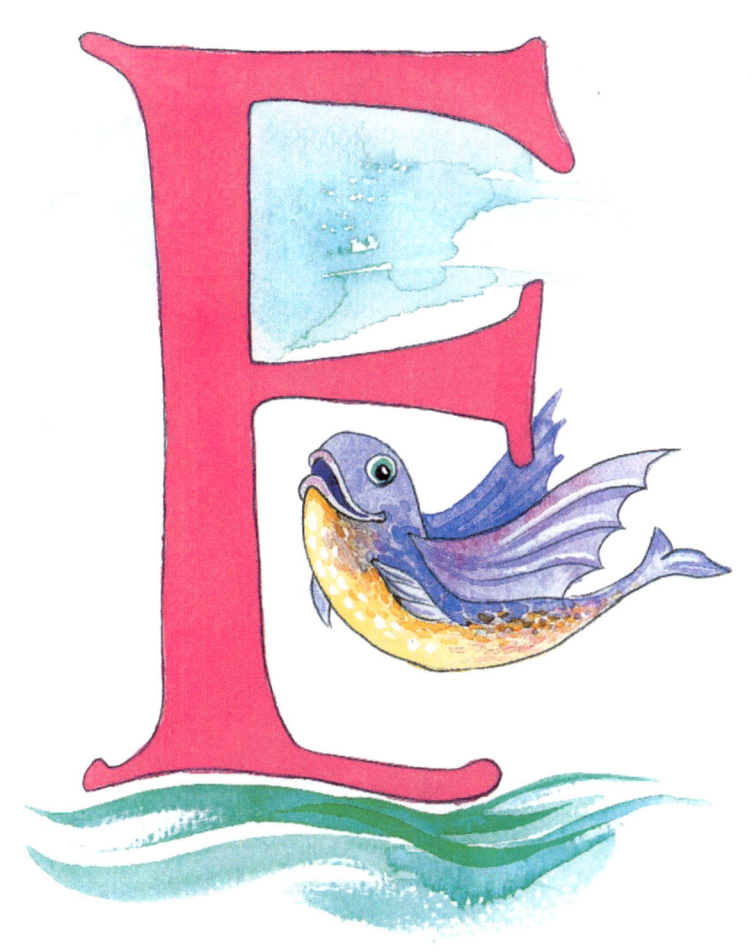

G is for giraffes

With necks graceful and long,

Grazing in trees

Where the birdies belong.

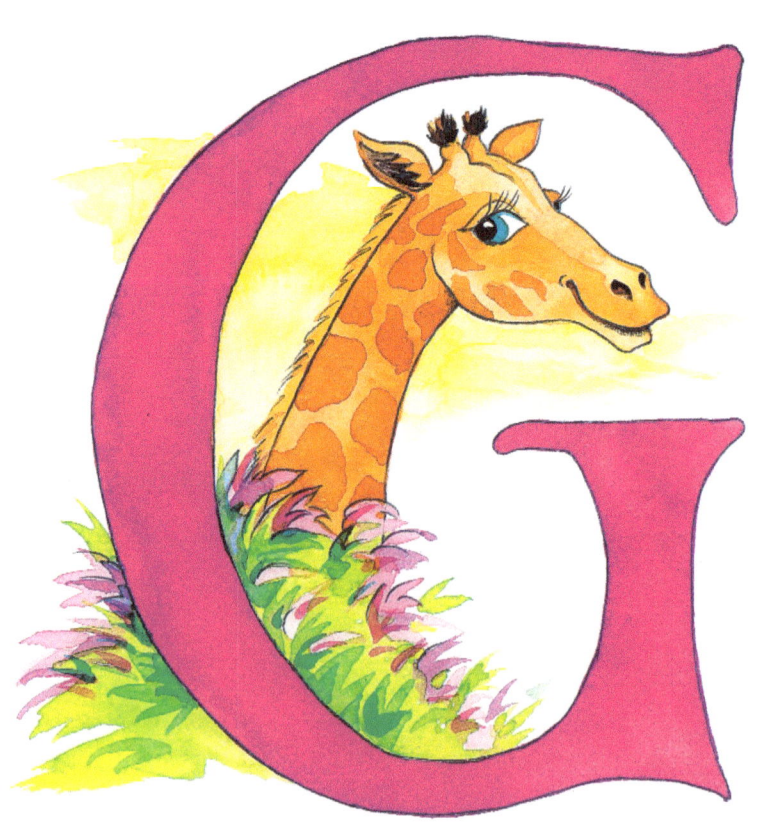

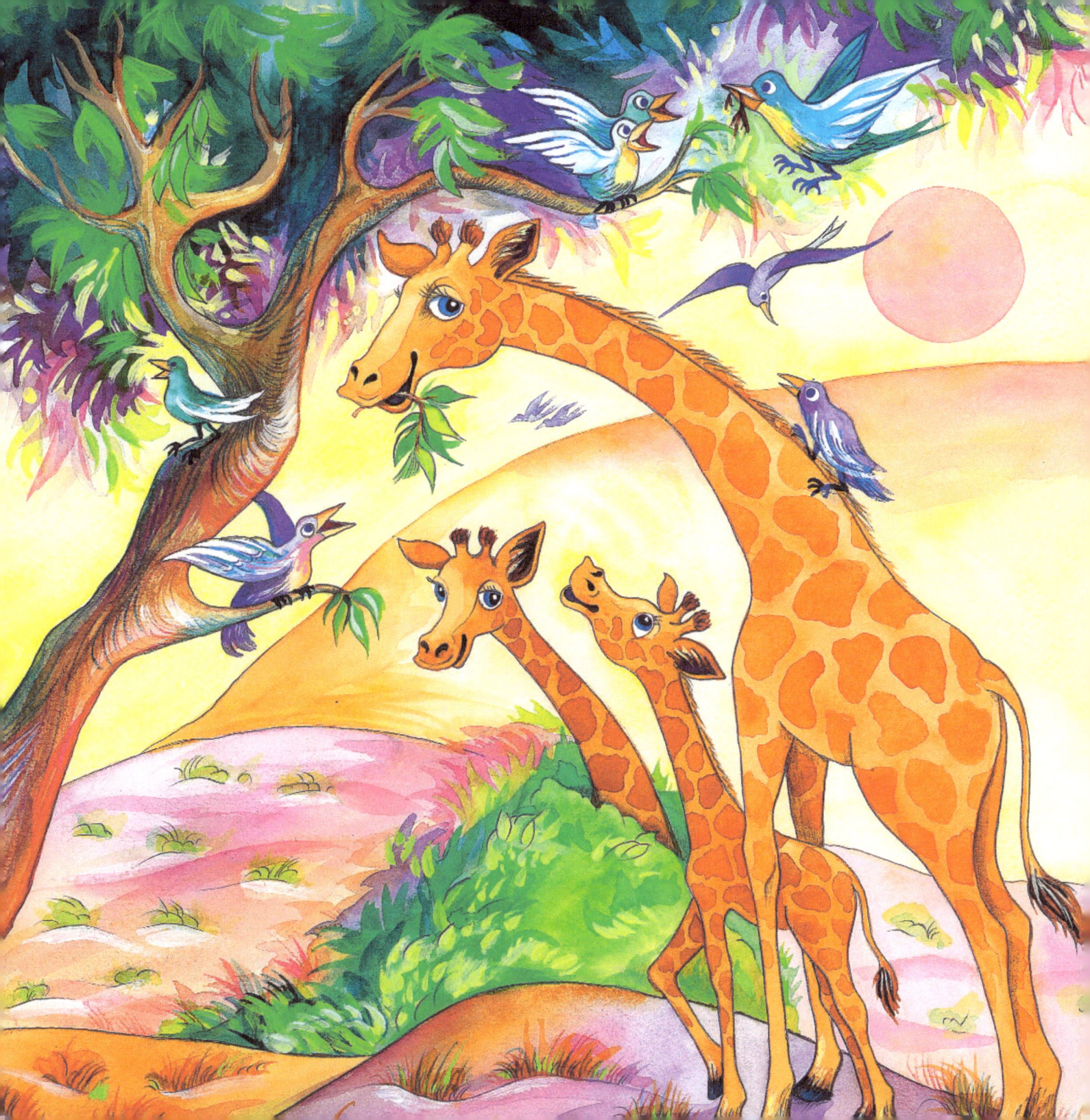

H is for hippo

Taking a peek

At a fish-eating heron

With a long pointy beak.

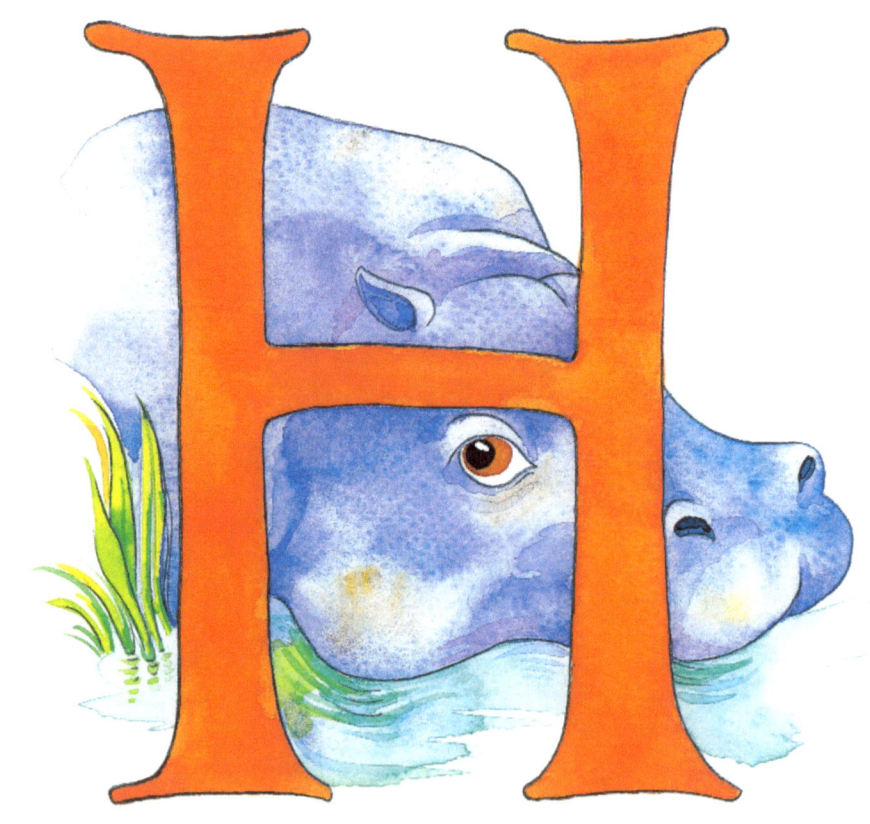

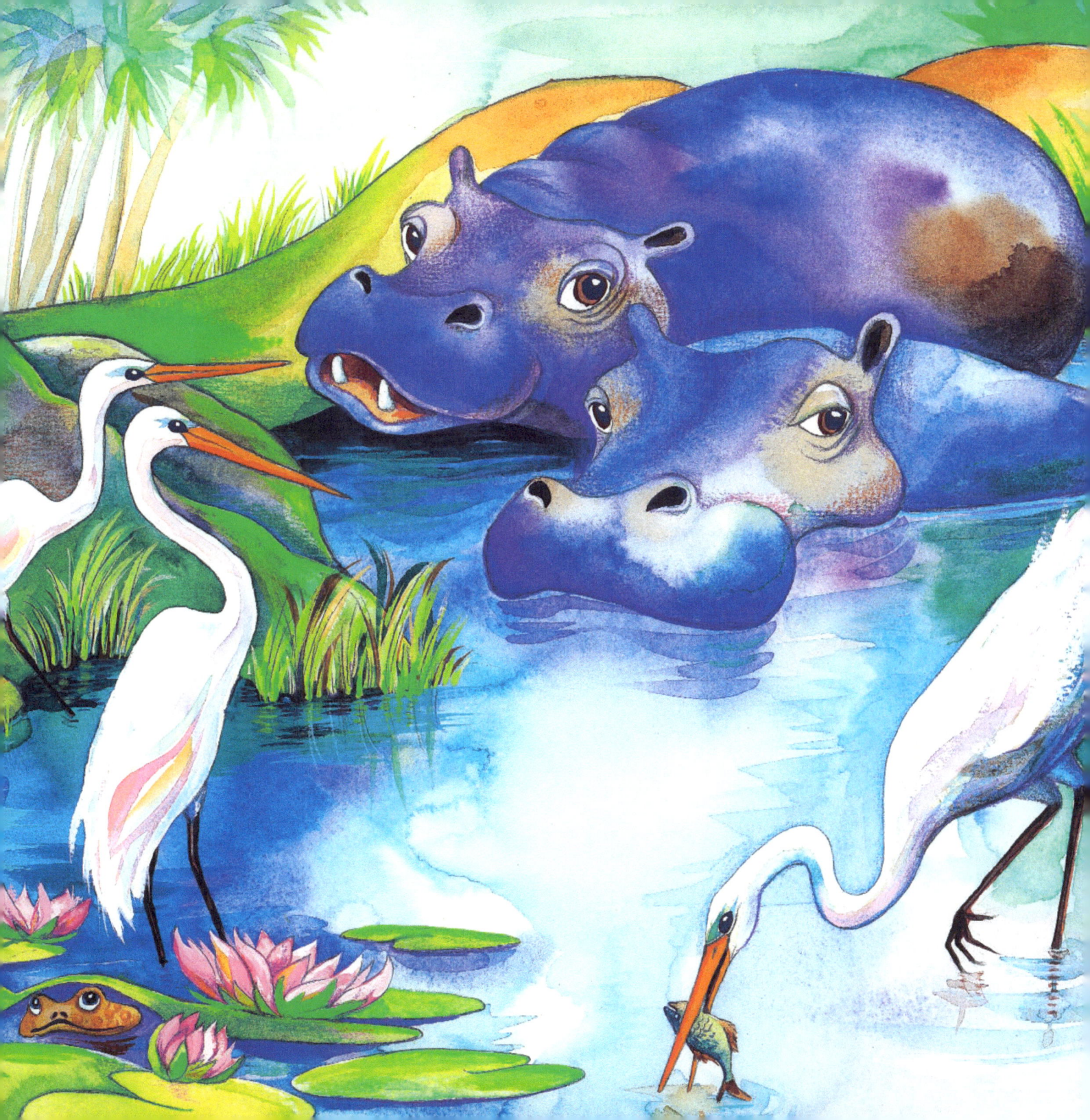

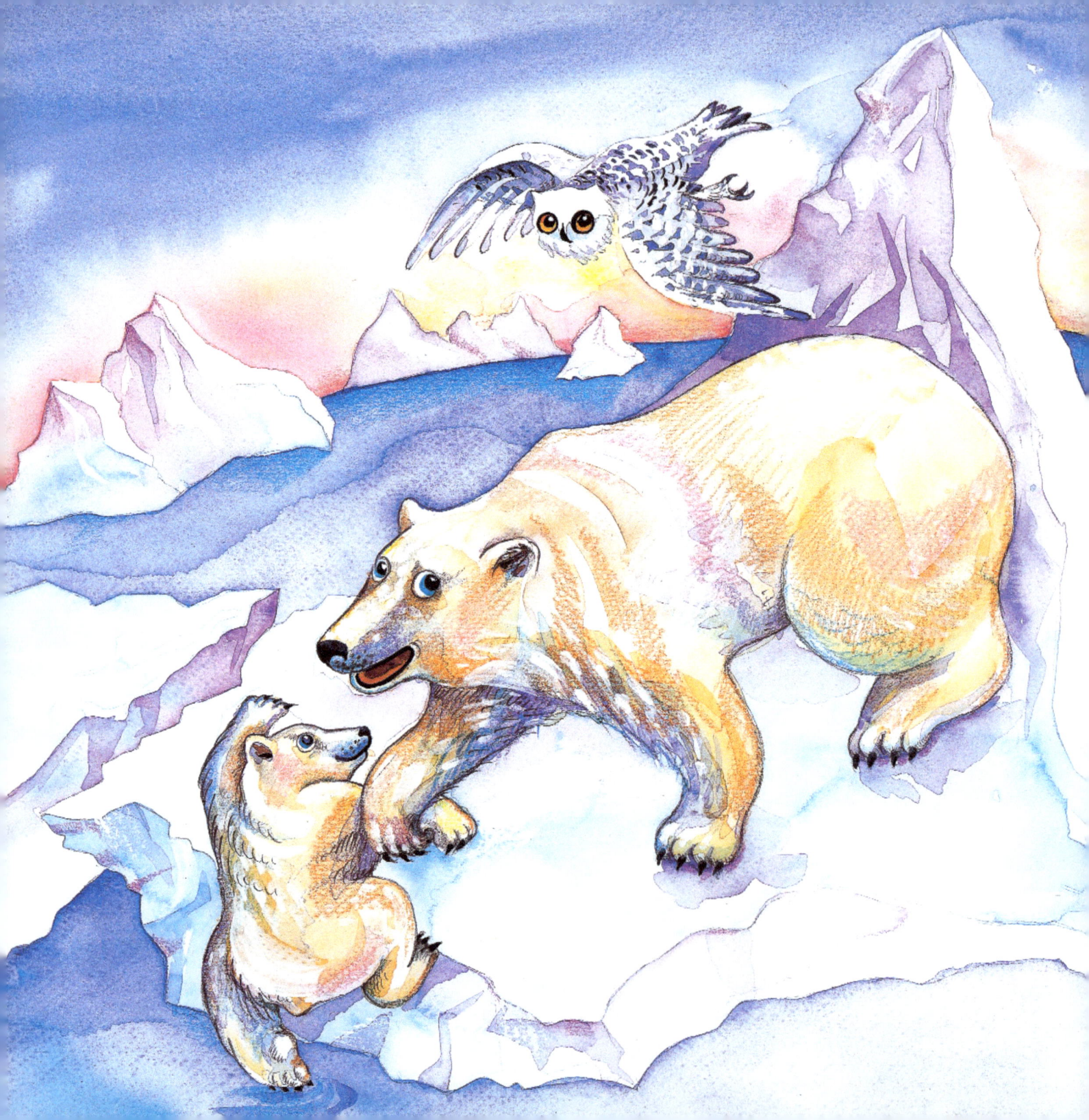

I is for iceberg,

An island of ice,

Where polar bears live

And find it quite nice.

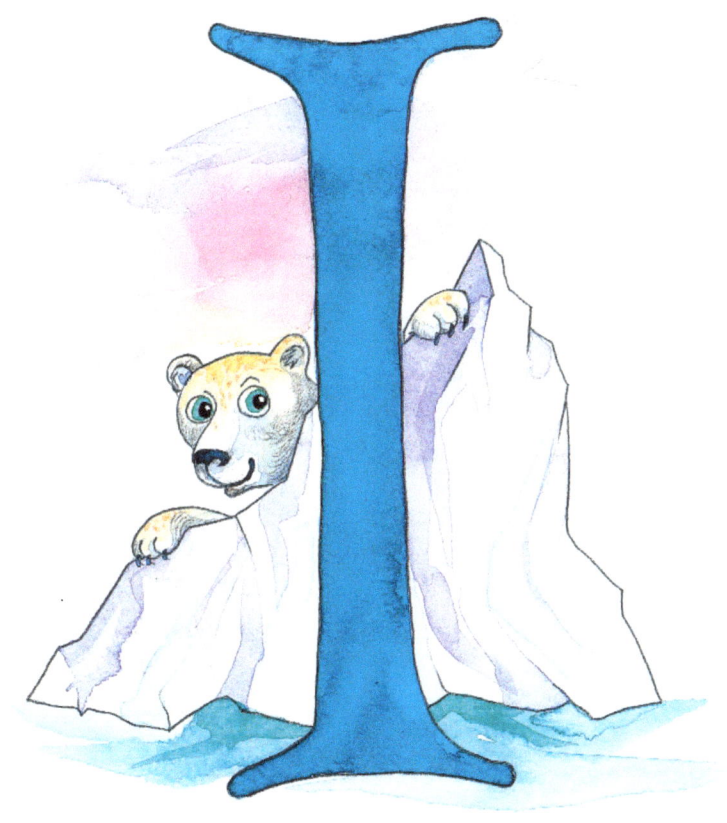

J is for jaguar

And jungle so green,

Where colorful monkeys

And birds can be seen.

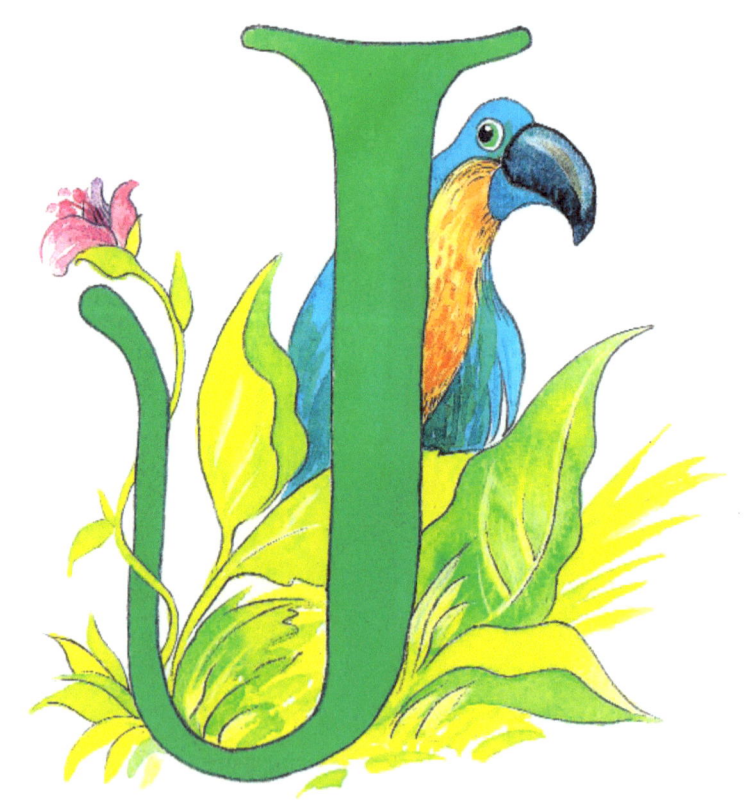

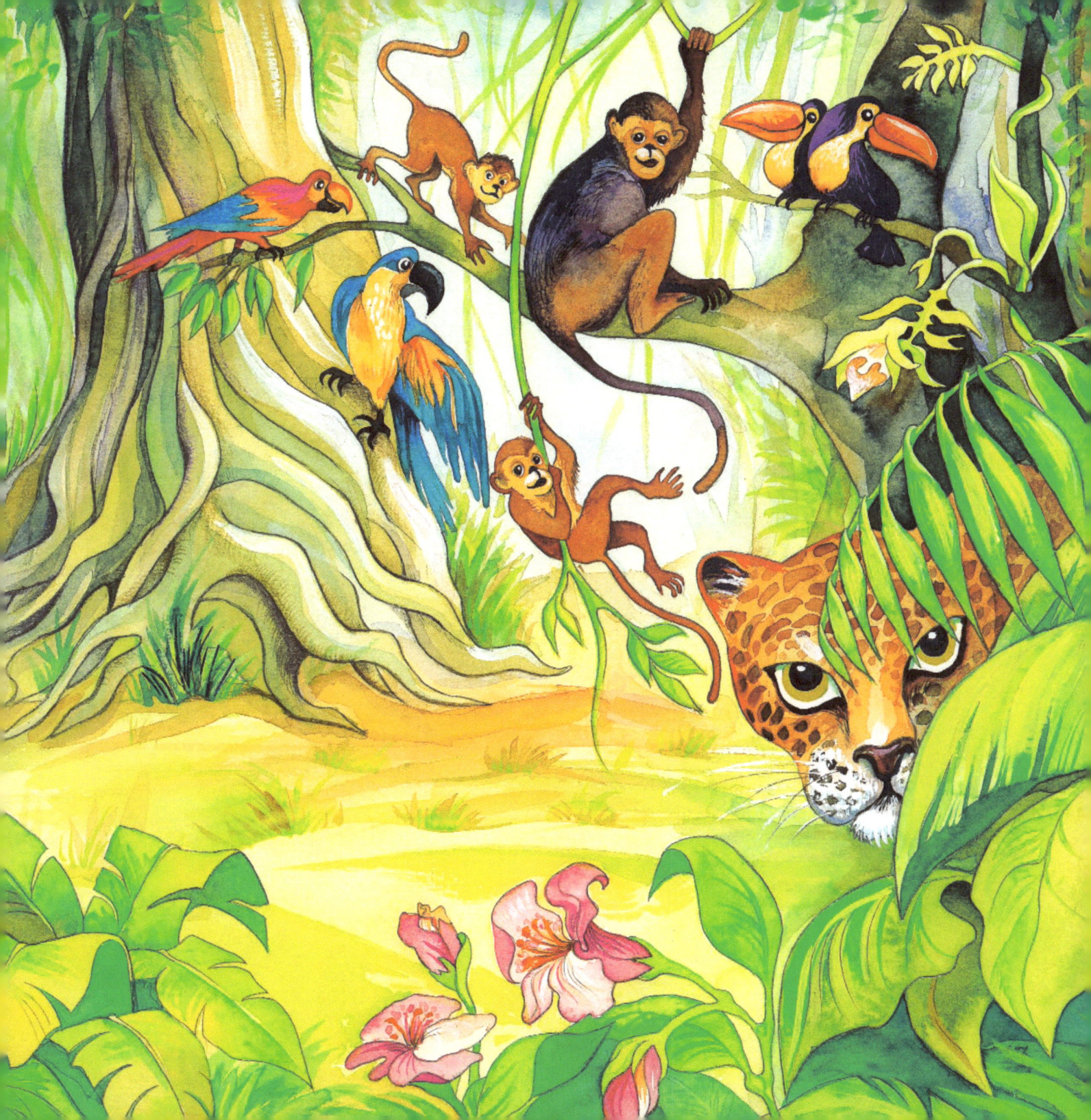

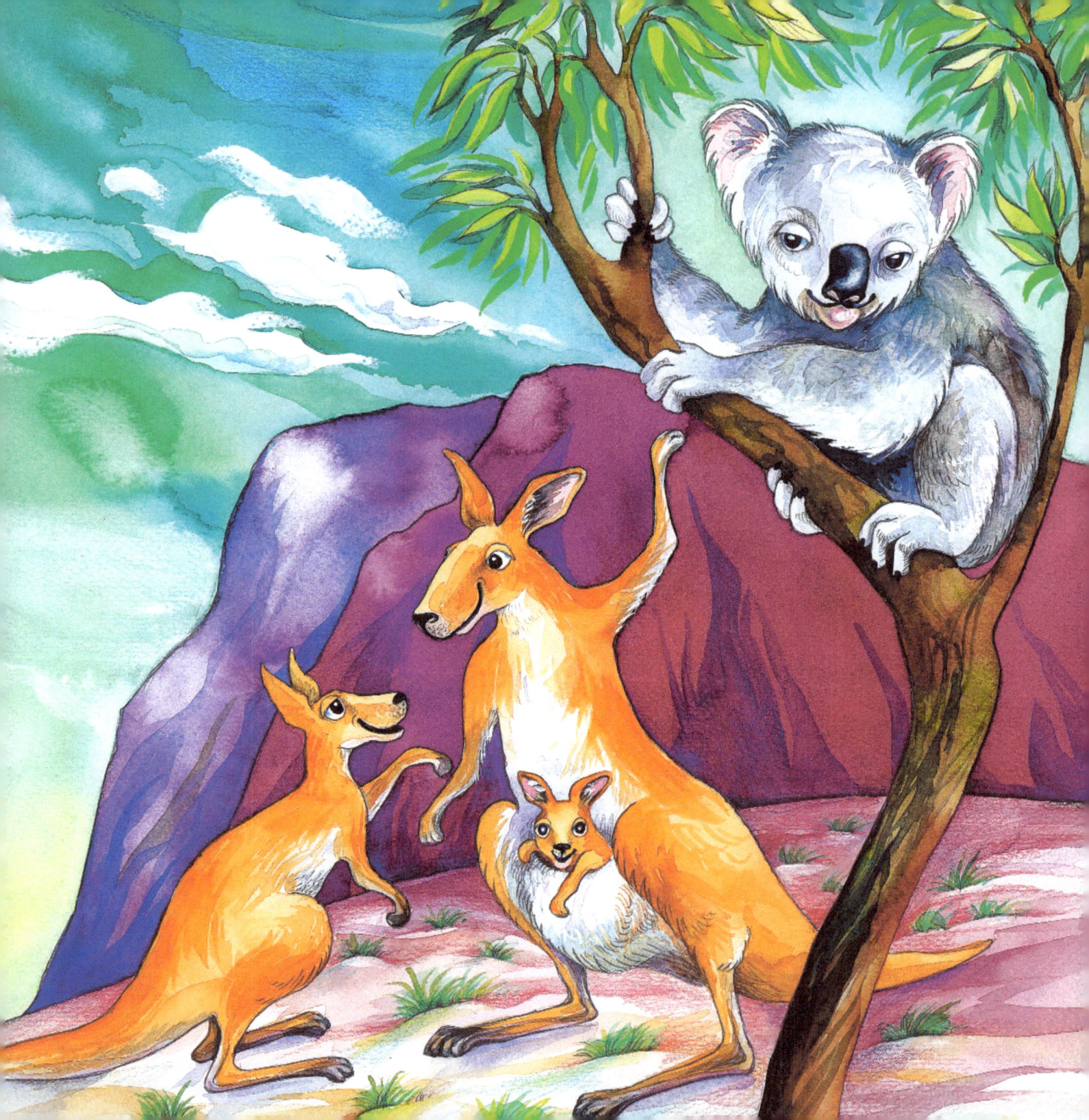

K is for koala,
Who lives in a tree,
And kangaroos, too –
Or do I see three?

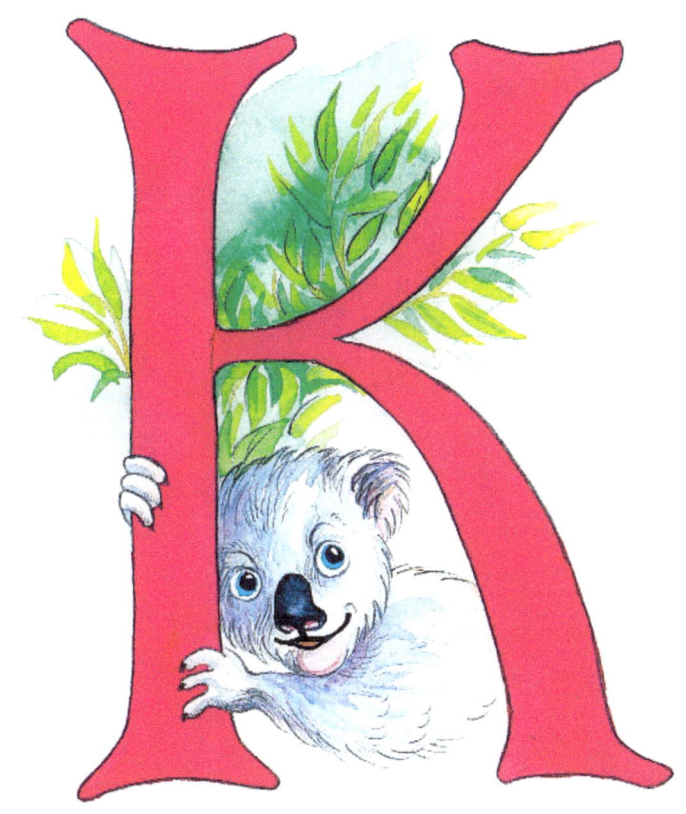

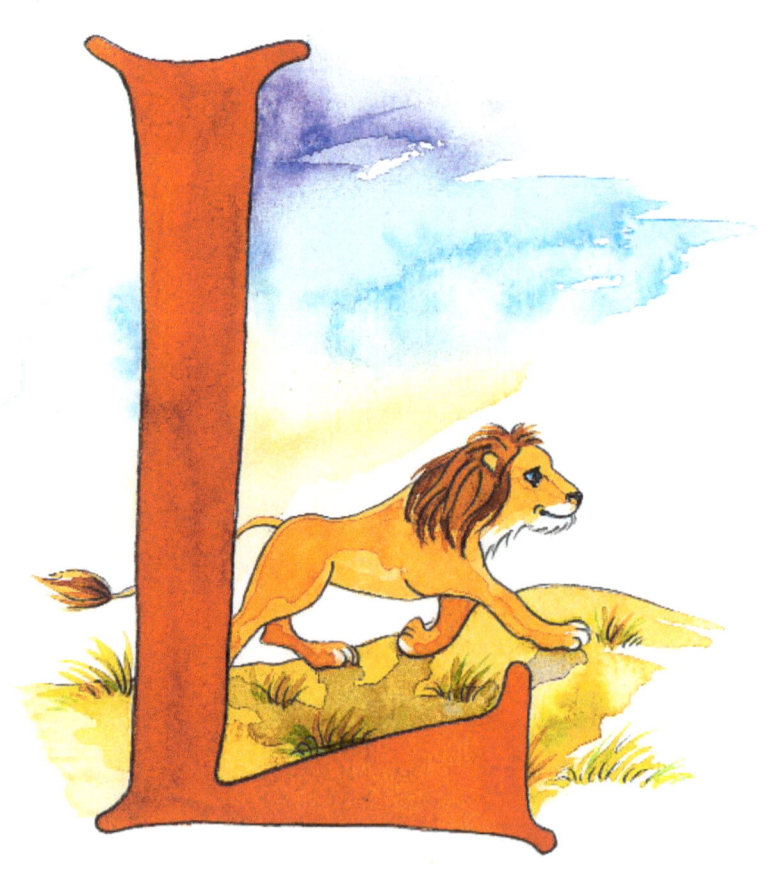

L is for lion,

The king of the beasts,

Lazily lounging

In between feasts.

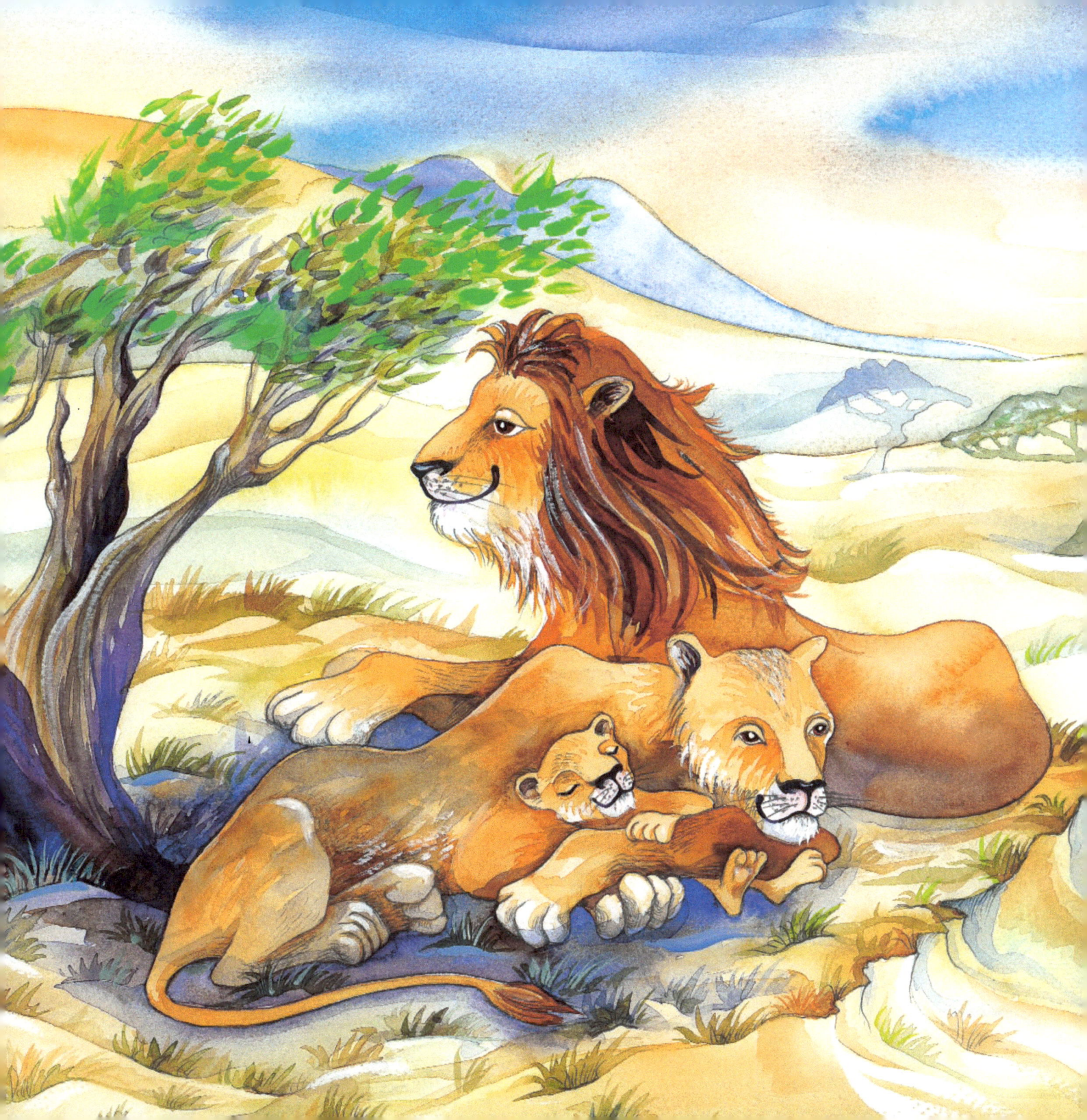

M is for mountains,

Jagged and steep,

Where goats have big horns –

And so do the sheep!

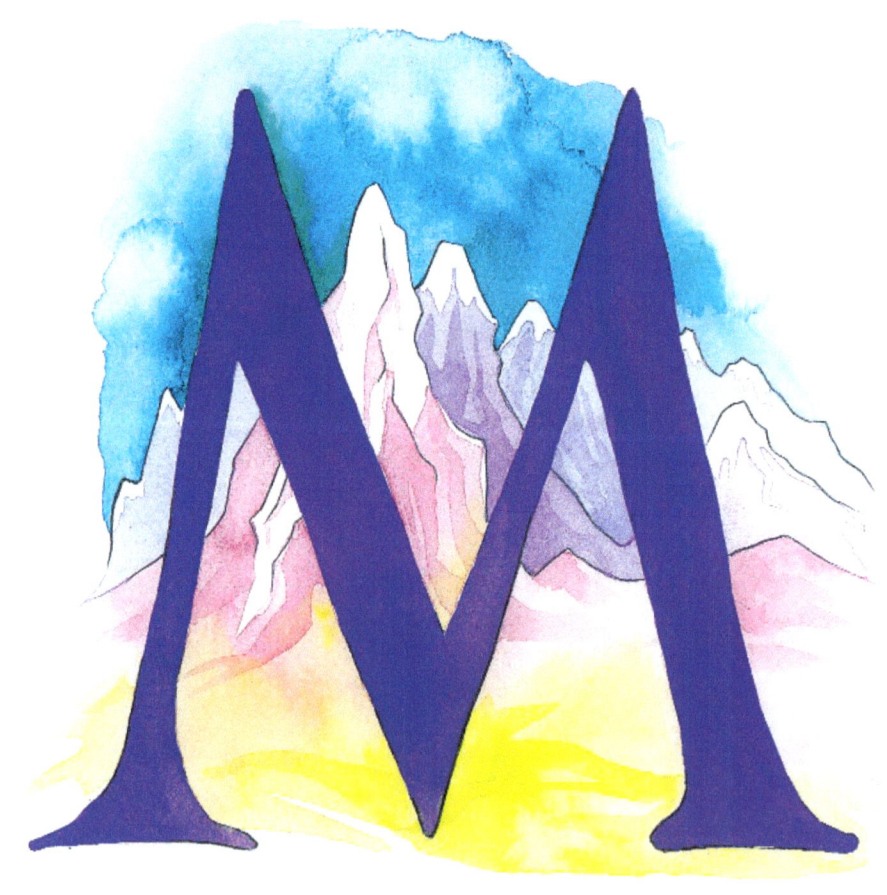

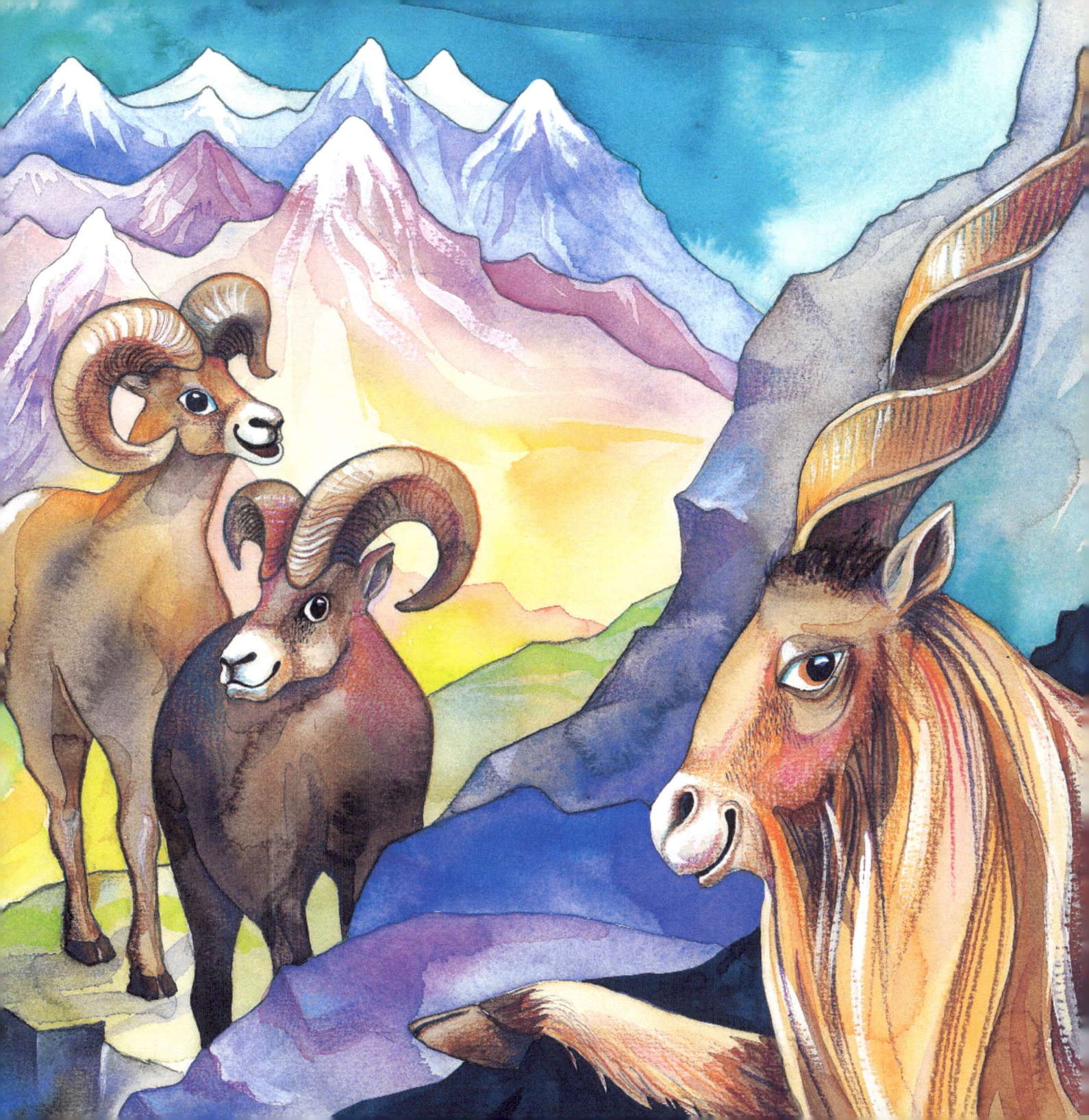

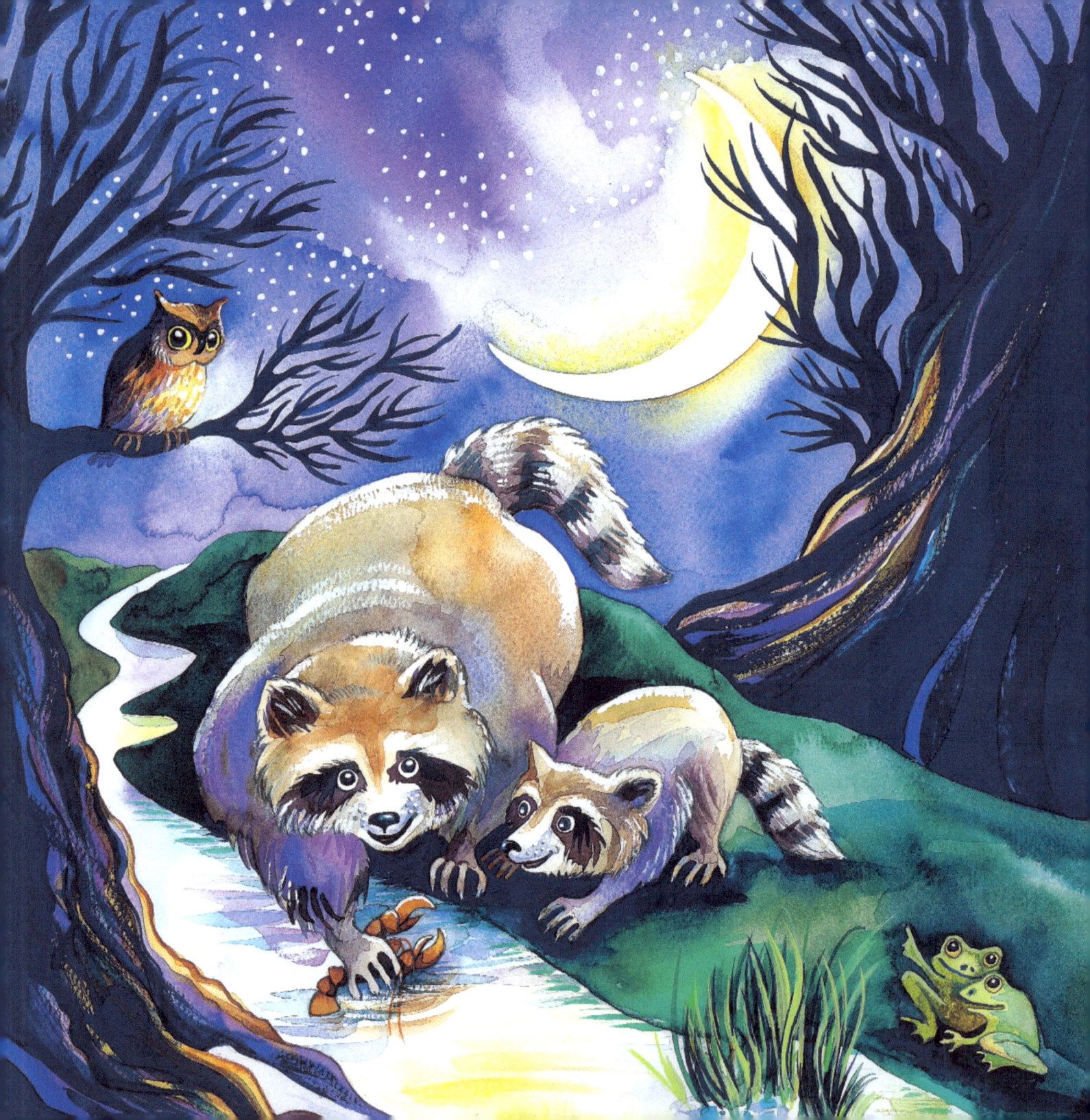

N is for night

And by the light of the moon,

You may come across

A clever raccoon.

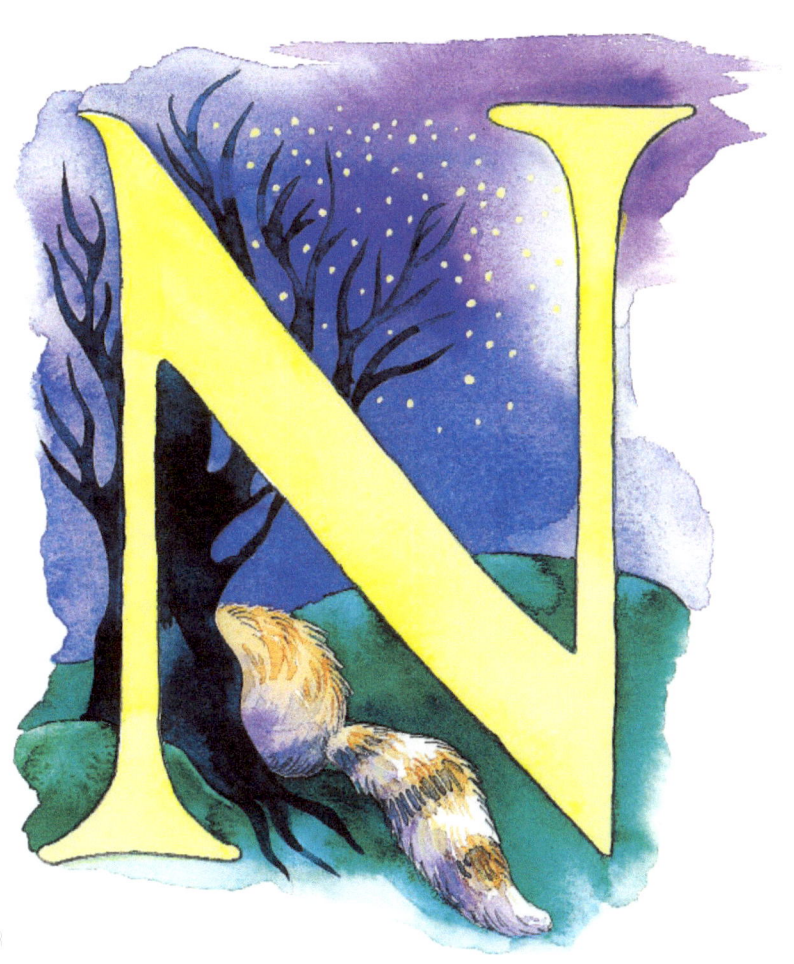

O is for ocean

Where deep down below,

Live some very odd creatures –

And most of them glow!

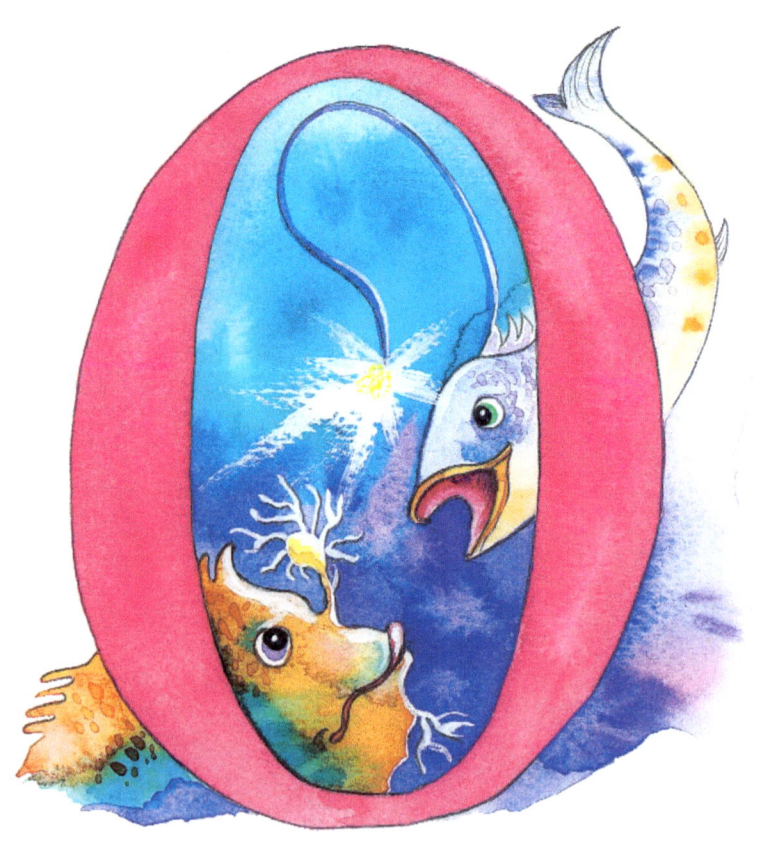

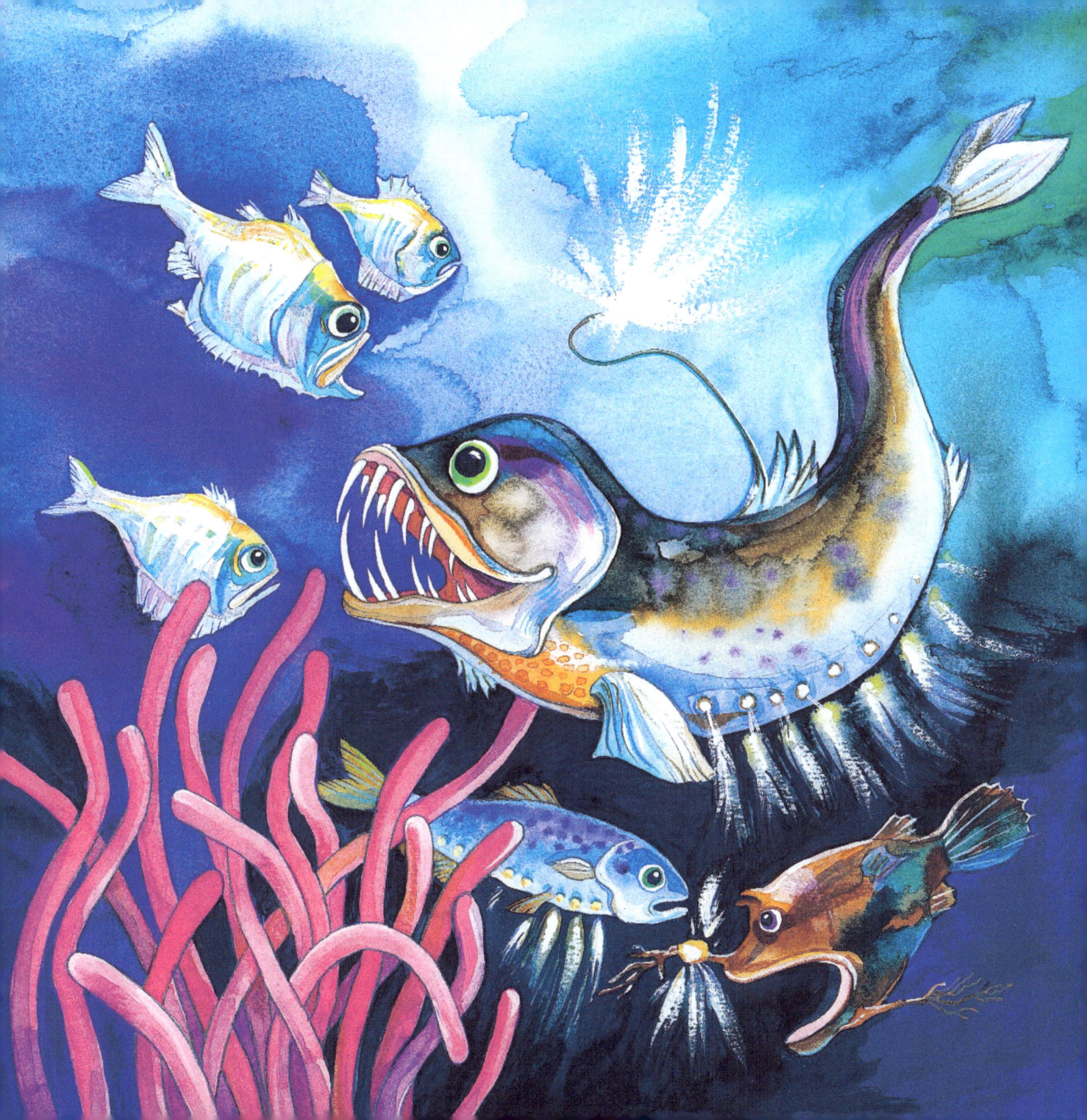

P is for panda

Chewing bamboo

And peacocks with plumes

Of green, purple, and blue.

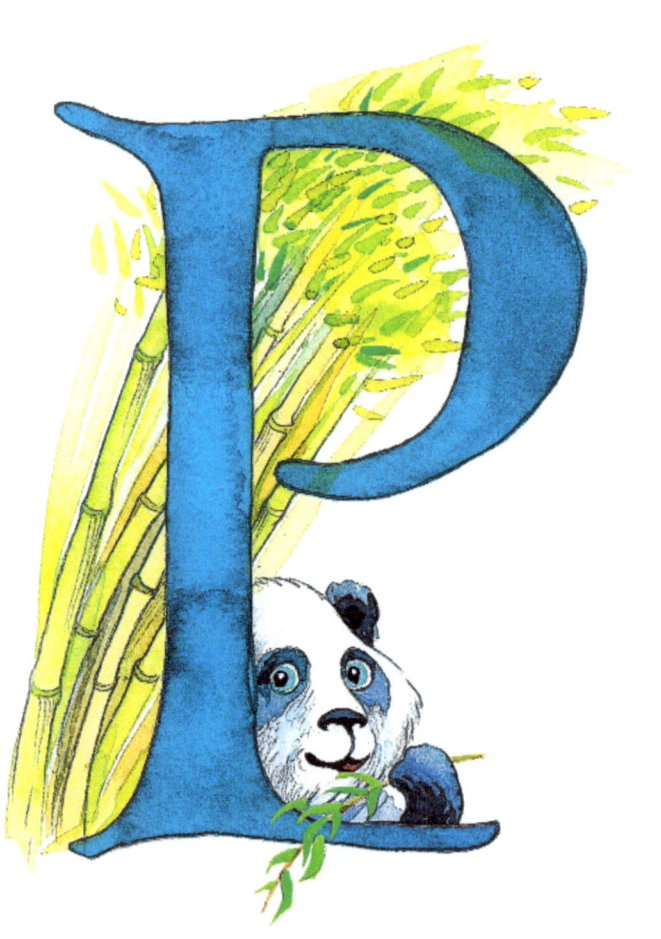

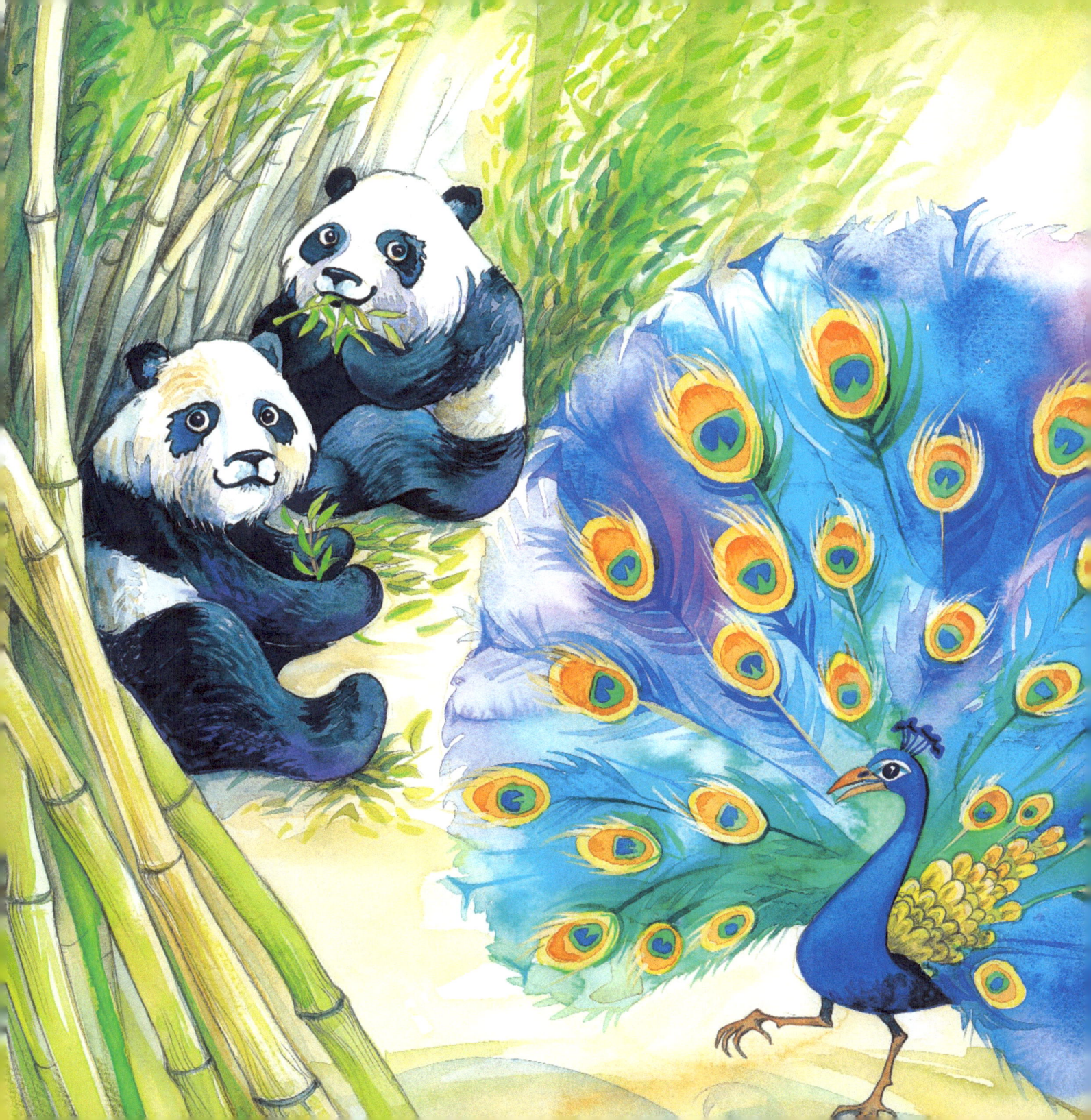

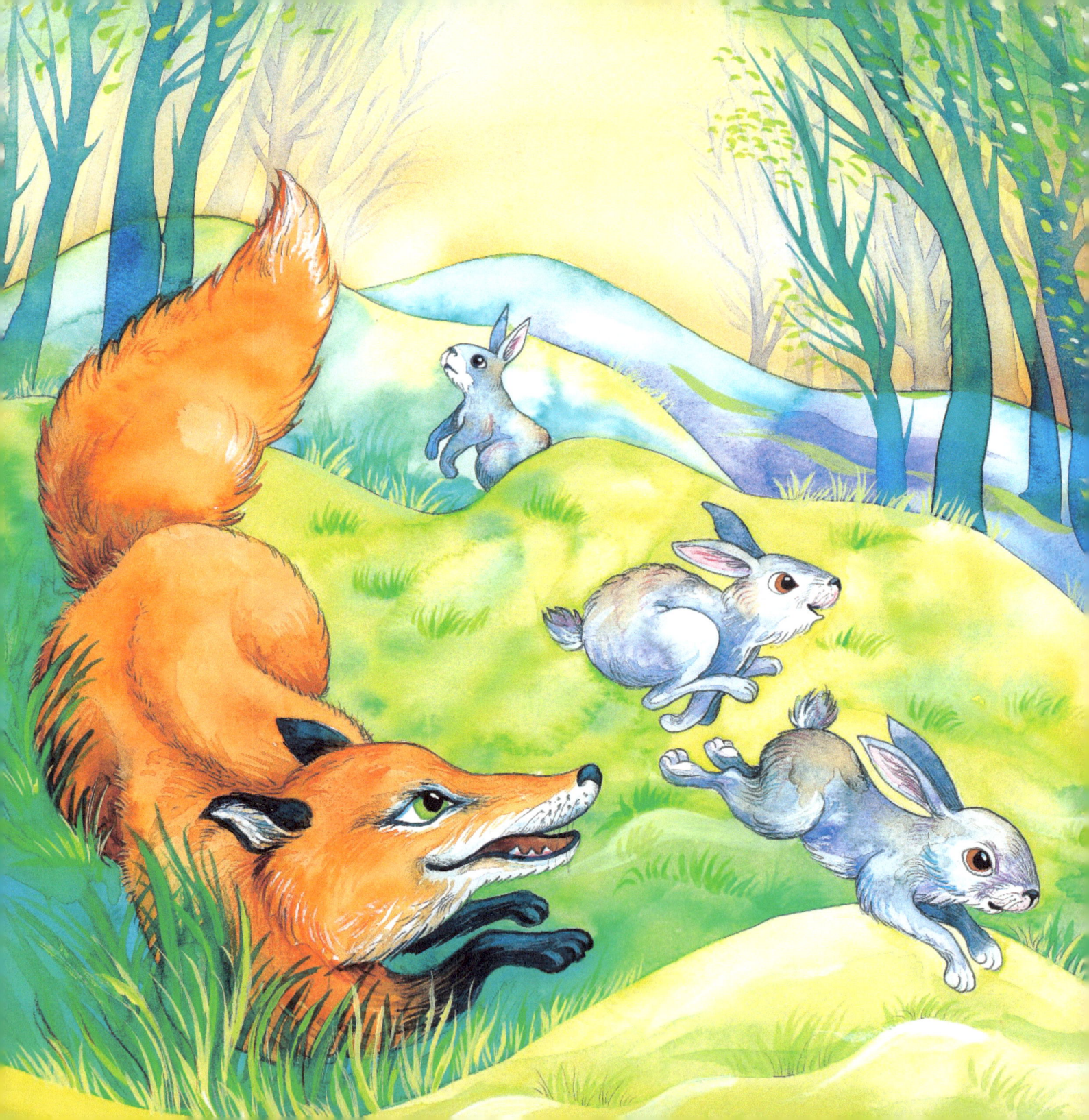

Q is for quick,

Which this hare better be,

He is chased by a fox

And he's got to get free!

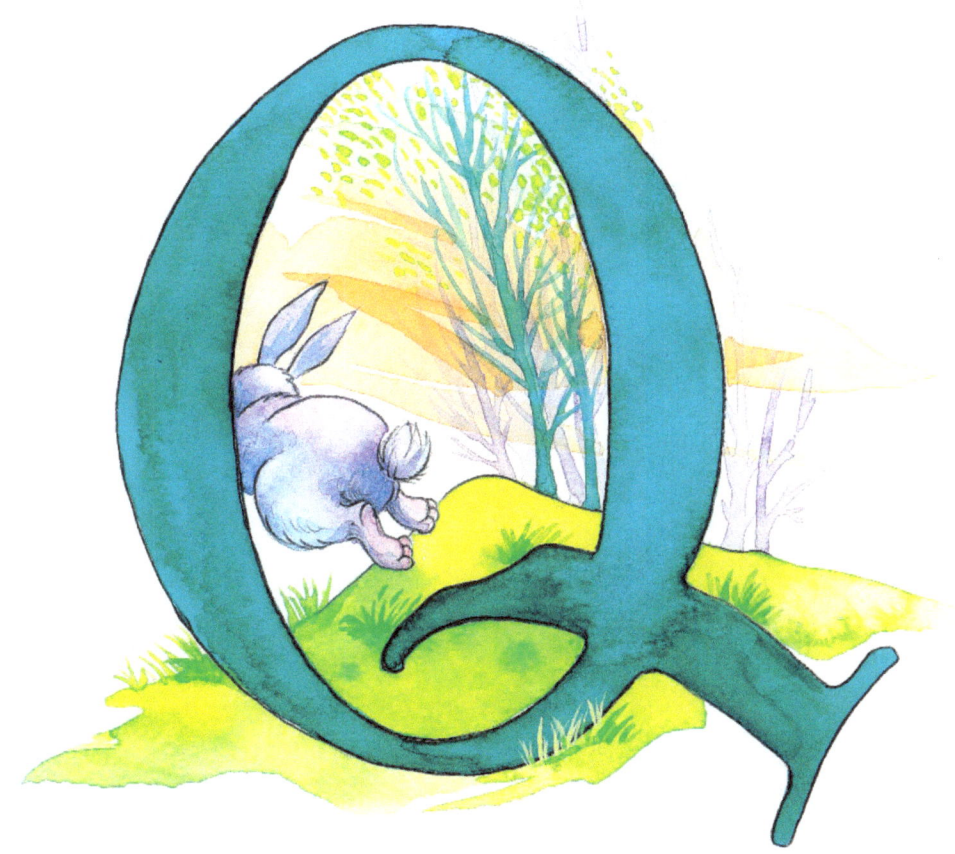

R is for reindeer

With antlers to wrangle,

Which sometimes wind up

In a bit of a tangle.

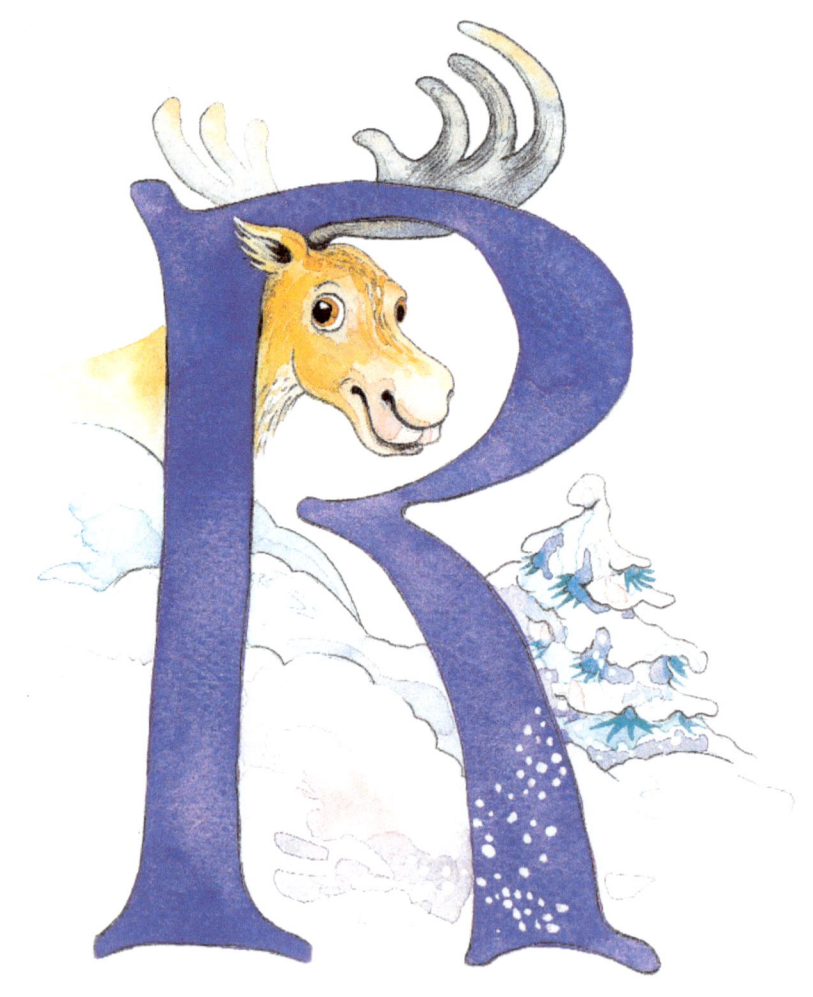

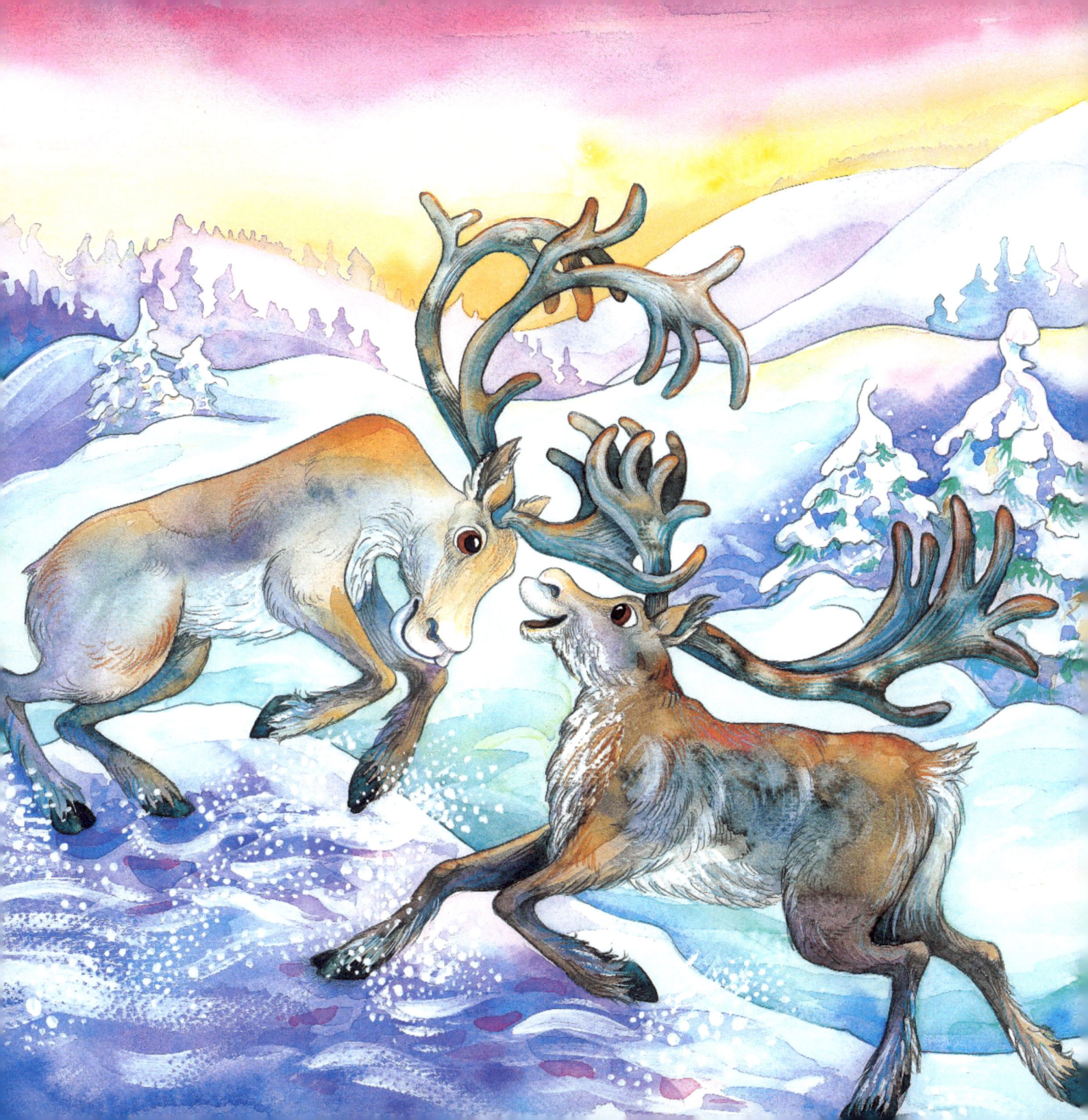

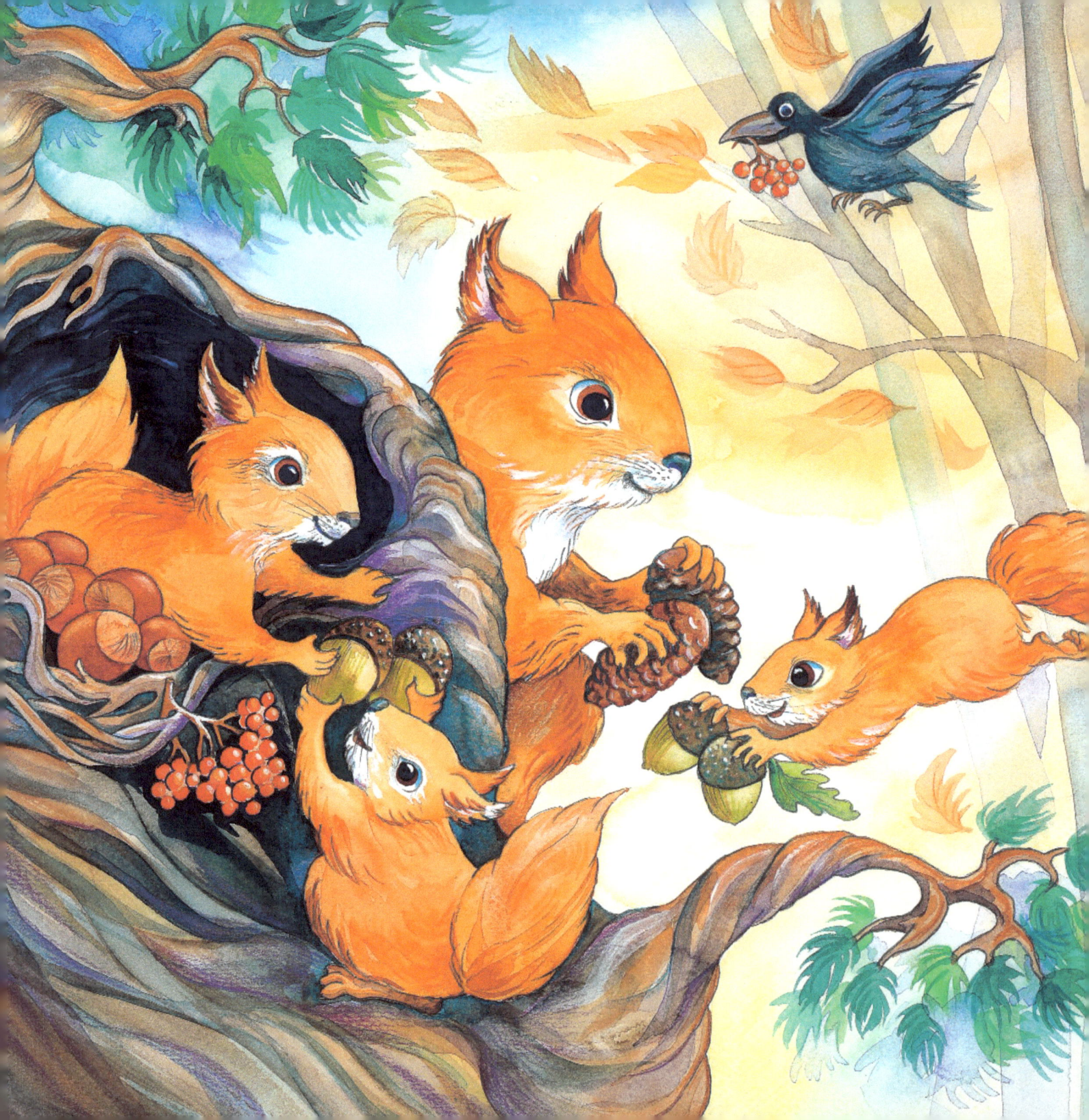

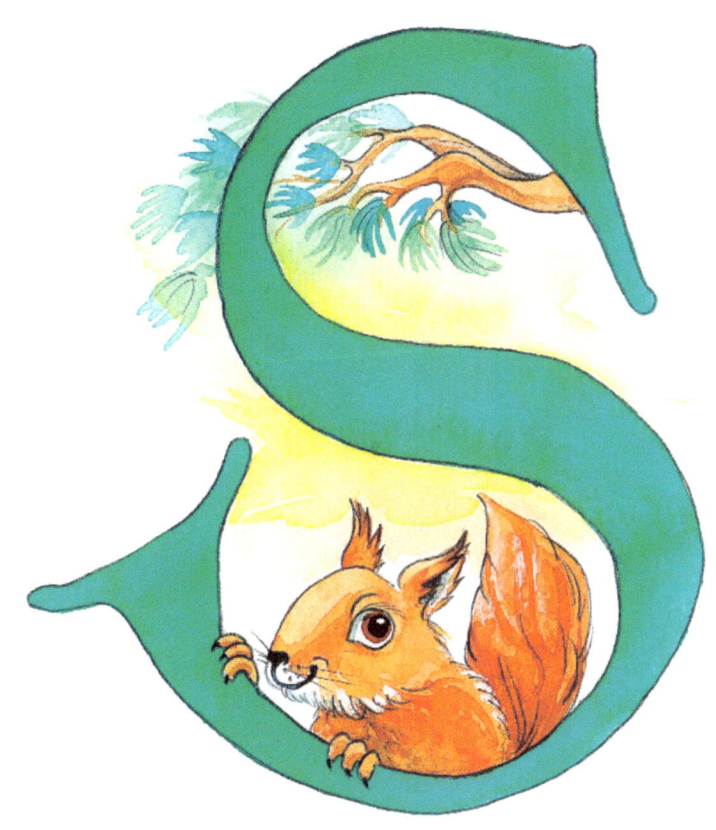

S is for squirrels

Stashing away

Acorns and nuts

For a cold winter day.

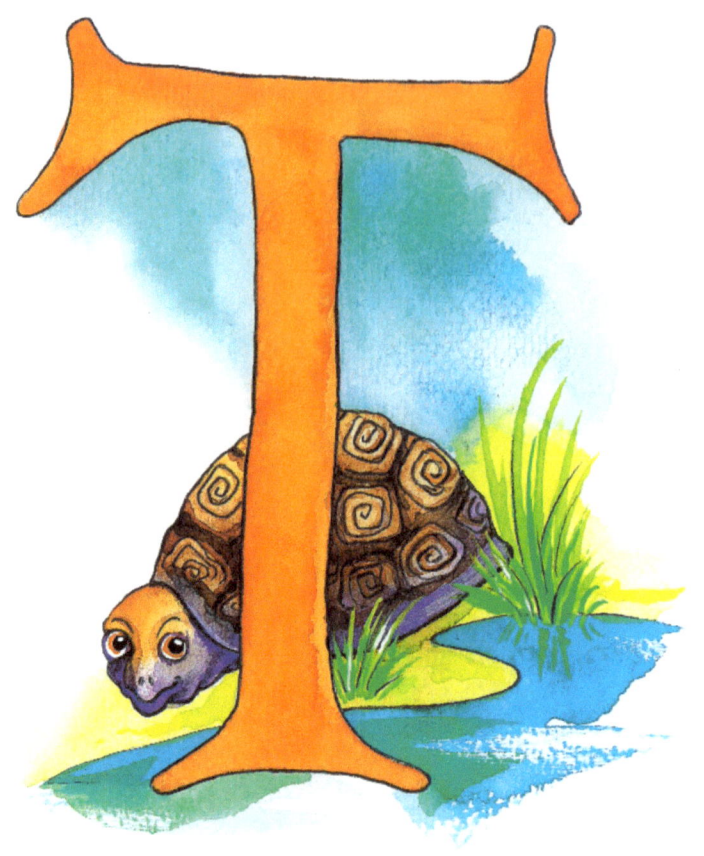

T is for tiger
Whom no one goes near,
Except for the turtle
With nothing to fear.

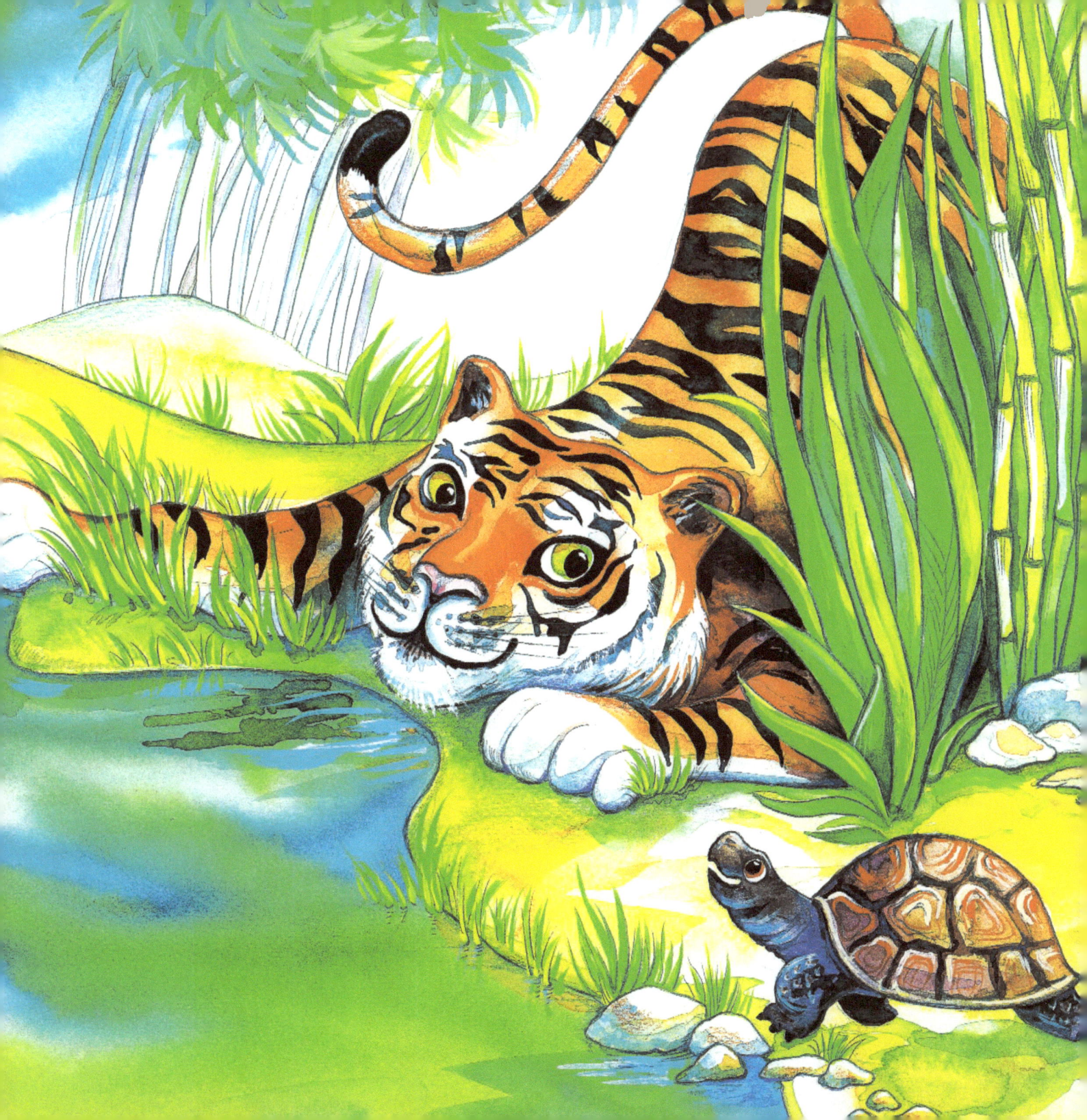

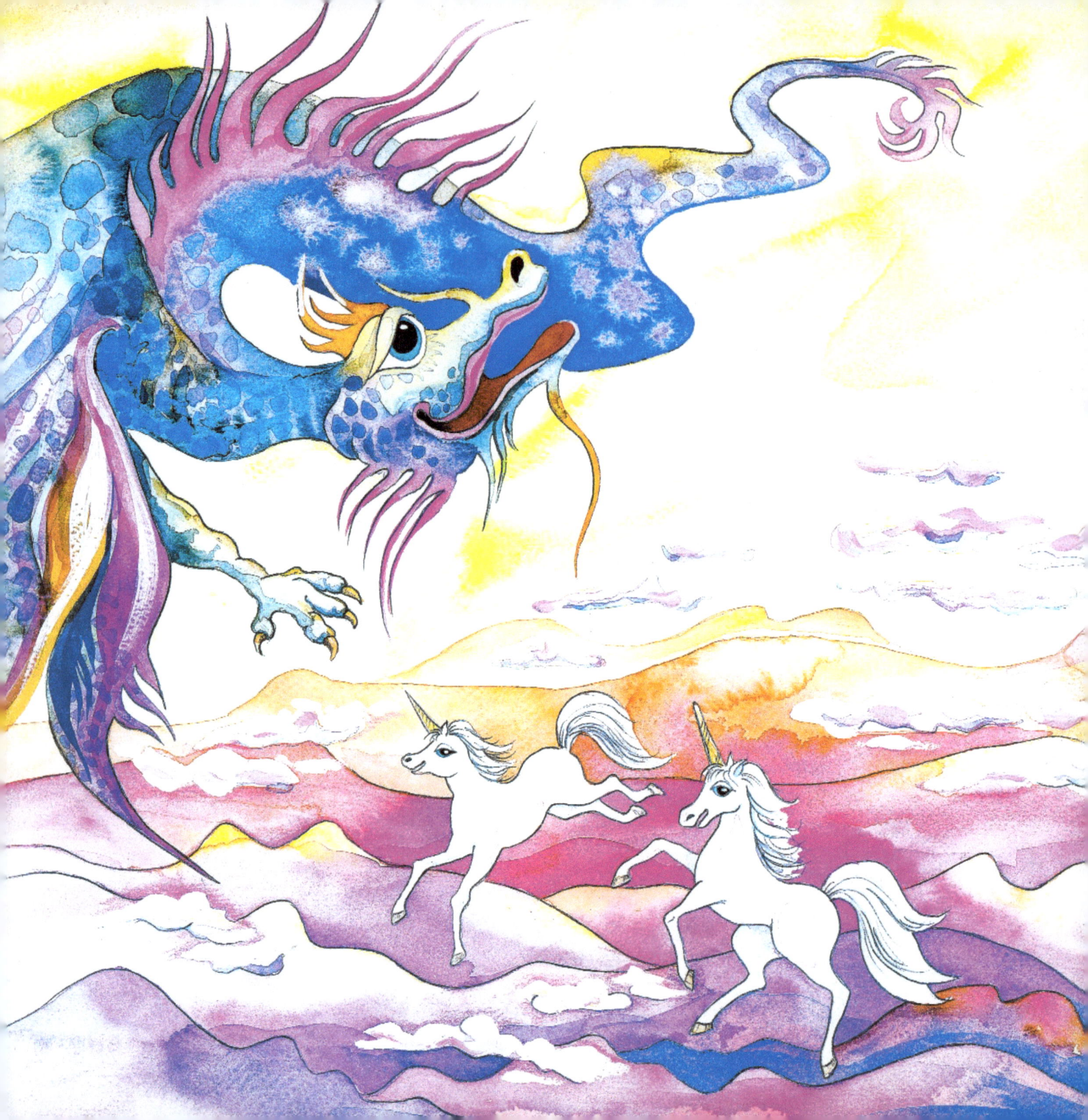

U is for unusual,

Untrue, and unseen,

Like dragons and unicorns –

If you know what I mean.

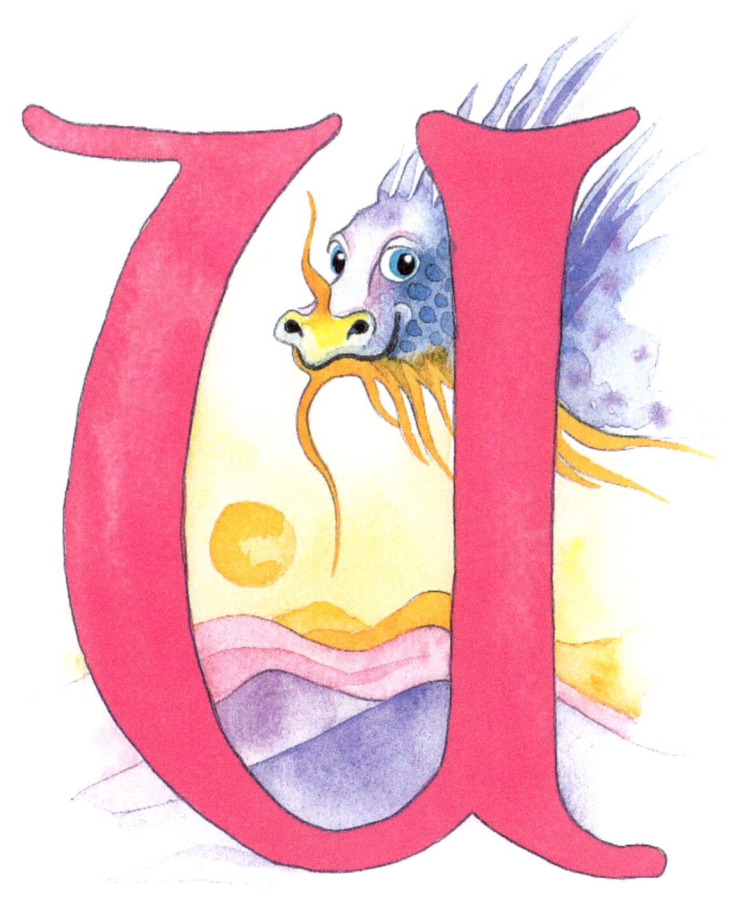

V is for viper

With venomous fangs

And vampire bat

Who sleeps while he hangs.

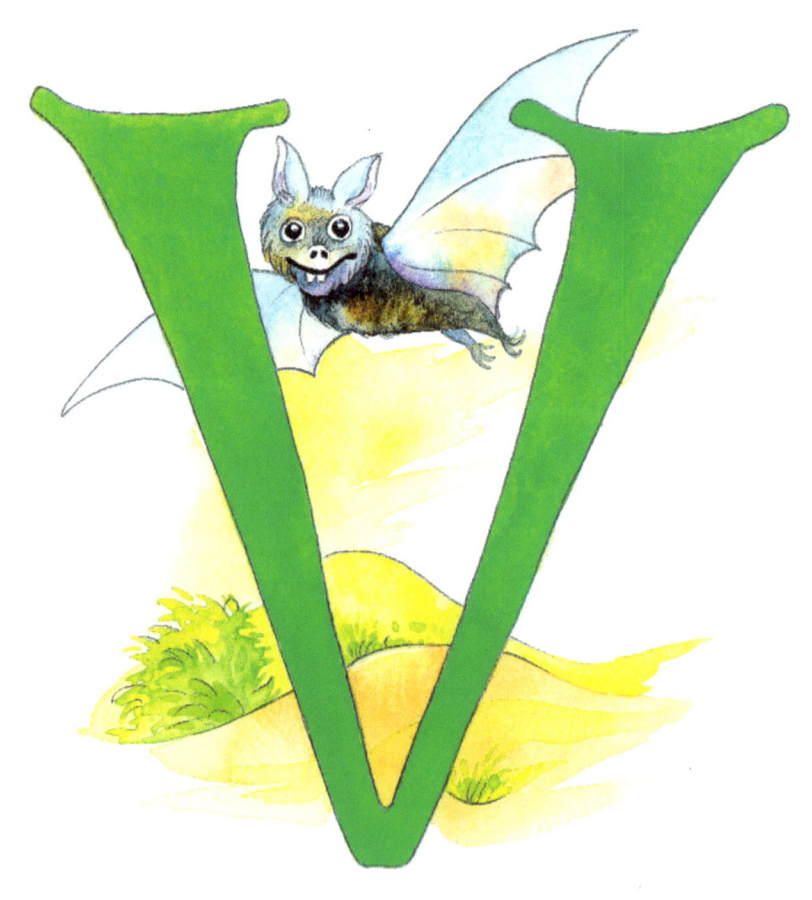

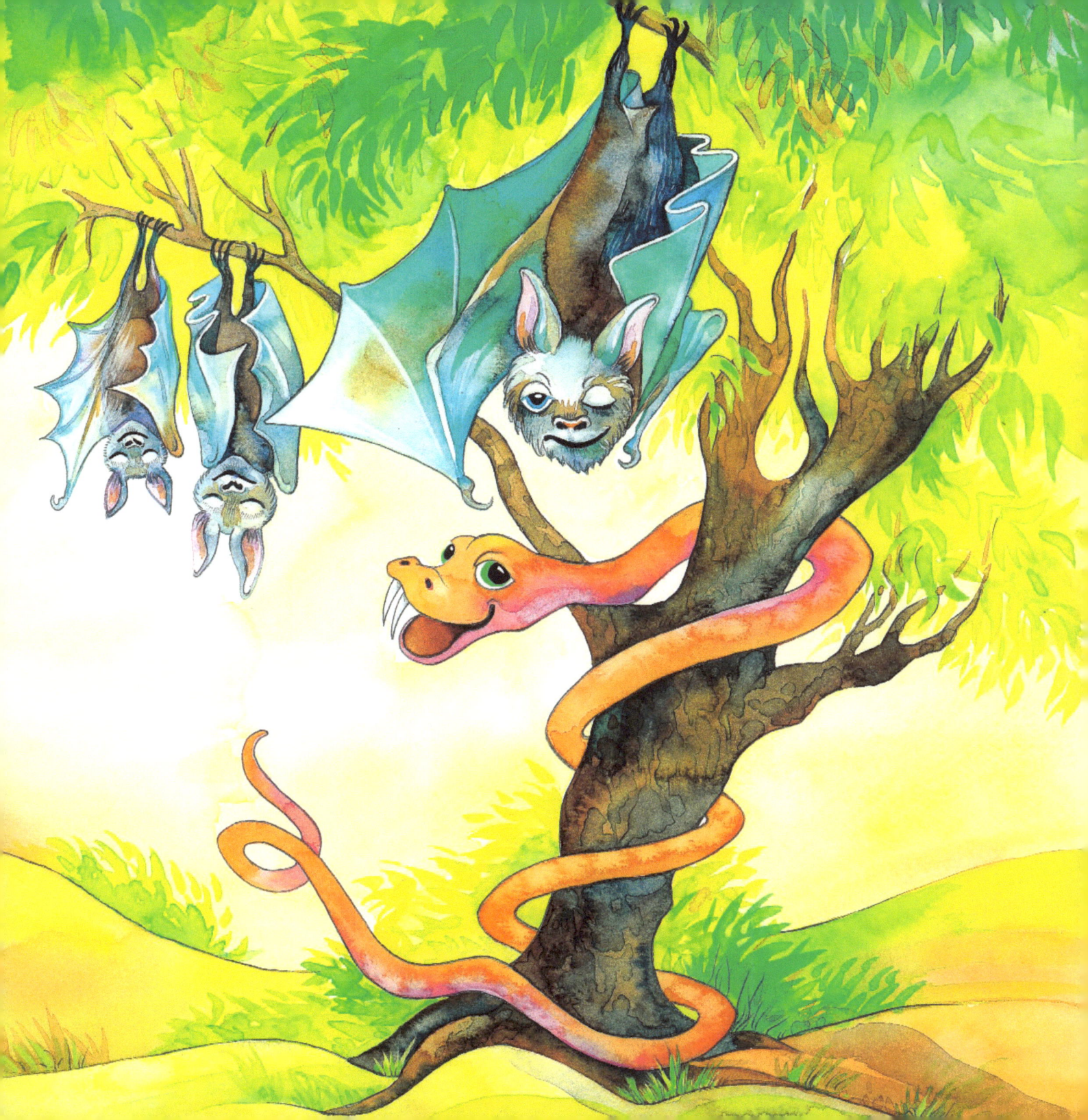

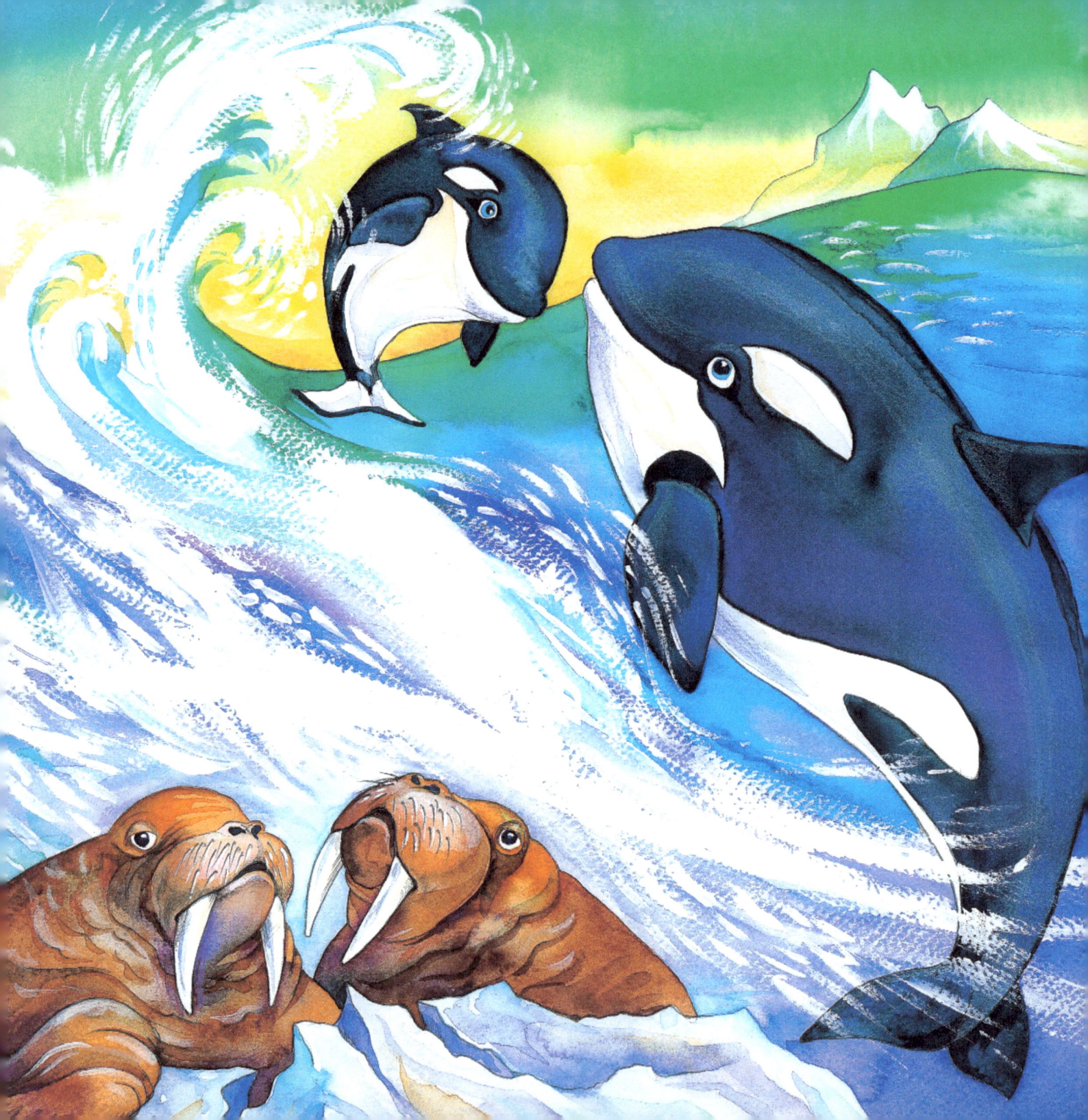

W is for walrus

And wonderful whales,

Who live undisturbed

By winter's rough gales.

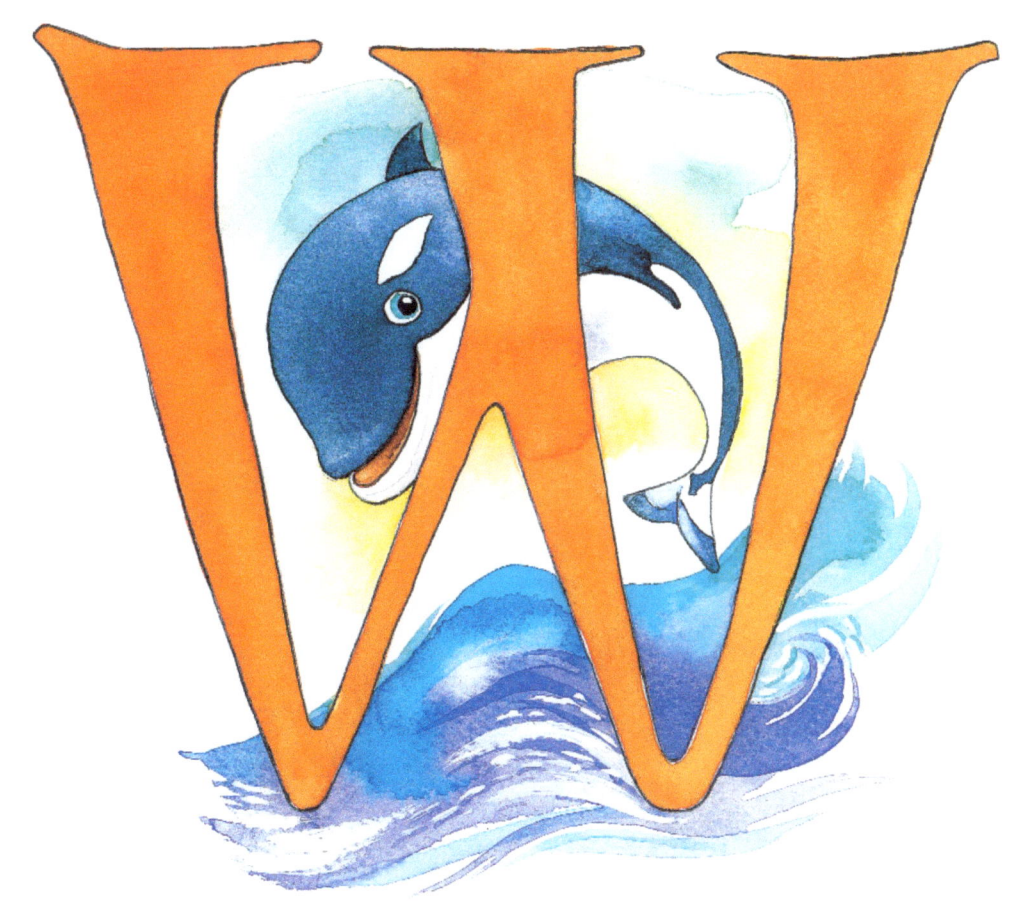

X is in extinct,

Which means gone and no more,

Such was the fate

Of the last dinosaur.

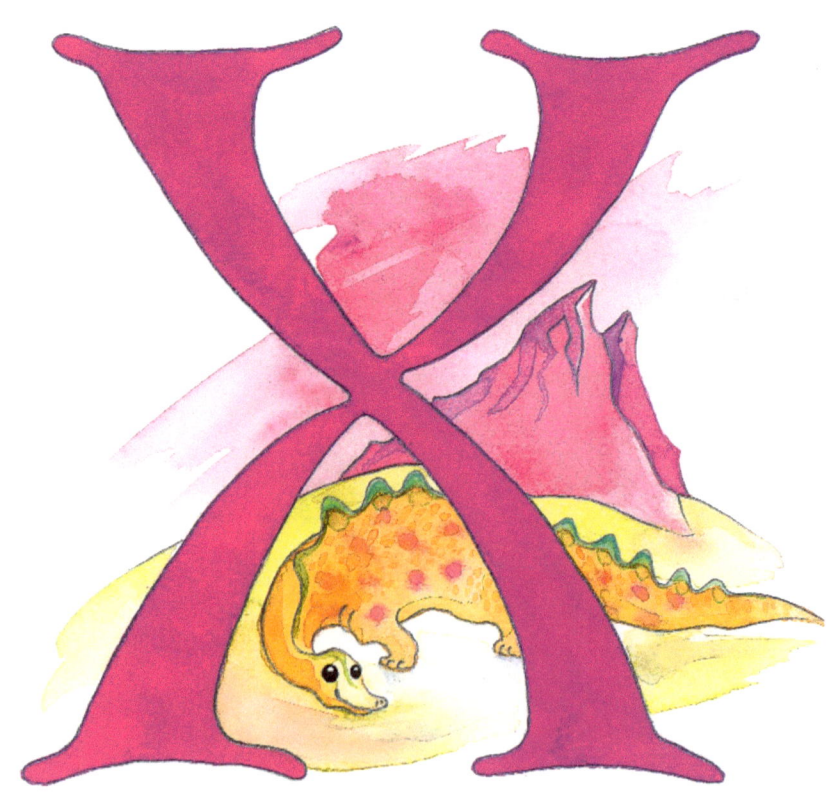

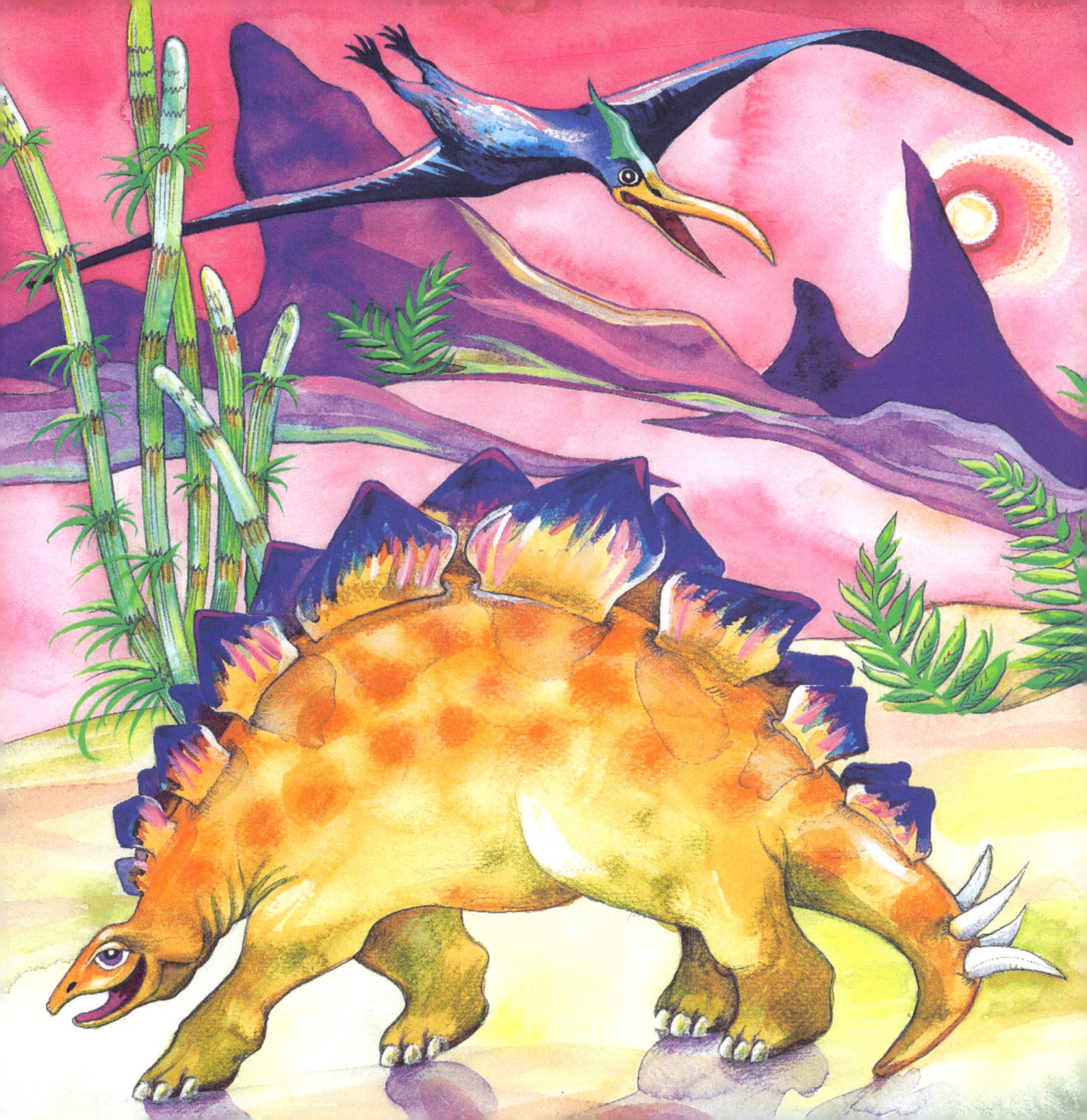

Y is for yeti

Whom no one has seen,

By leaving huge footprints

We know where he's been.

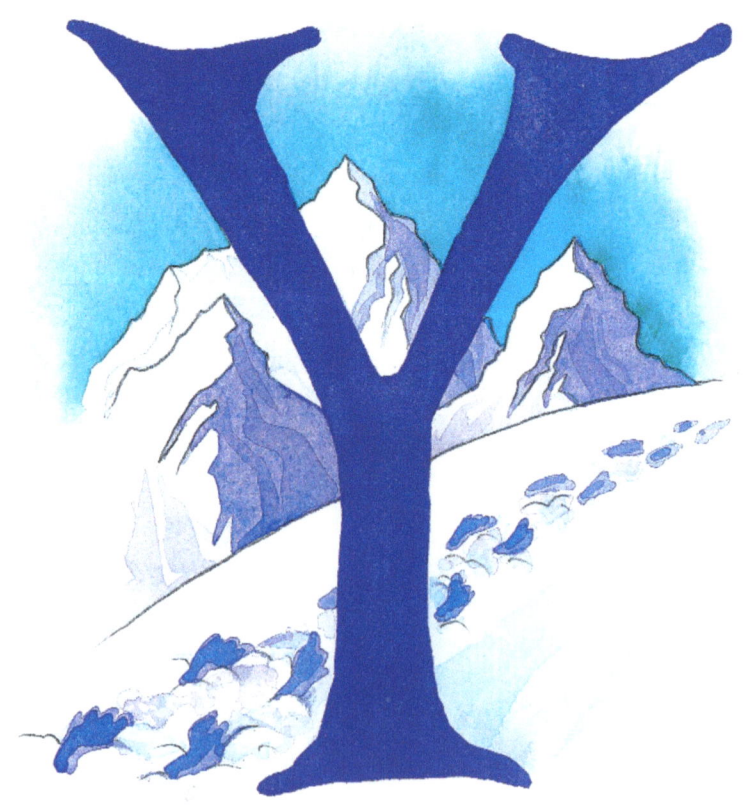

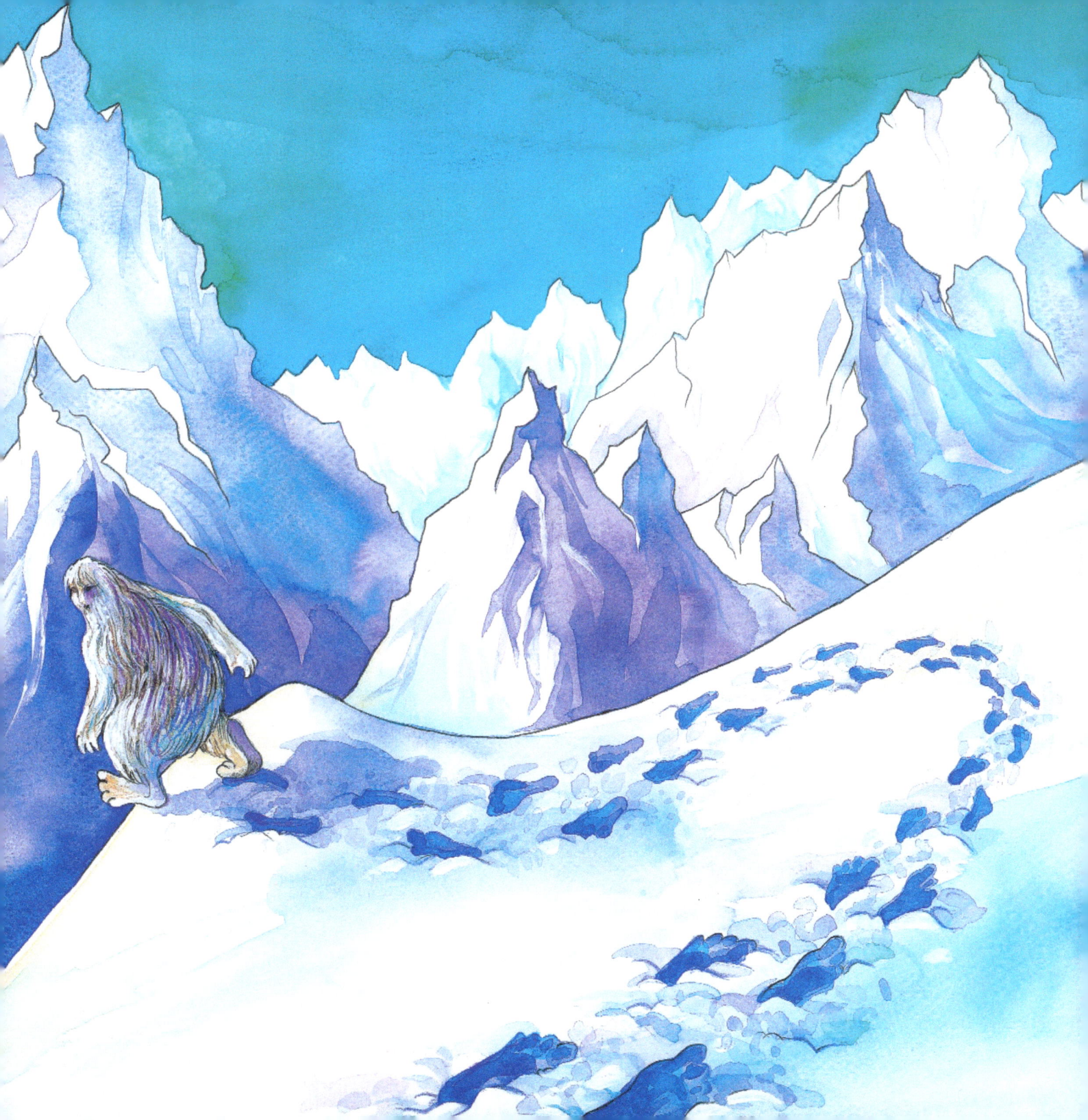

Z is the first letter

Of zebra and zebu,

If you want to see more,

You should go to the zoo!

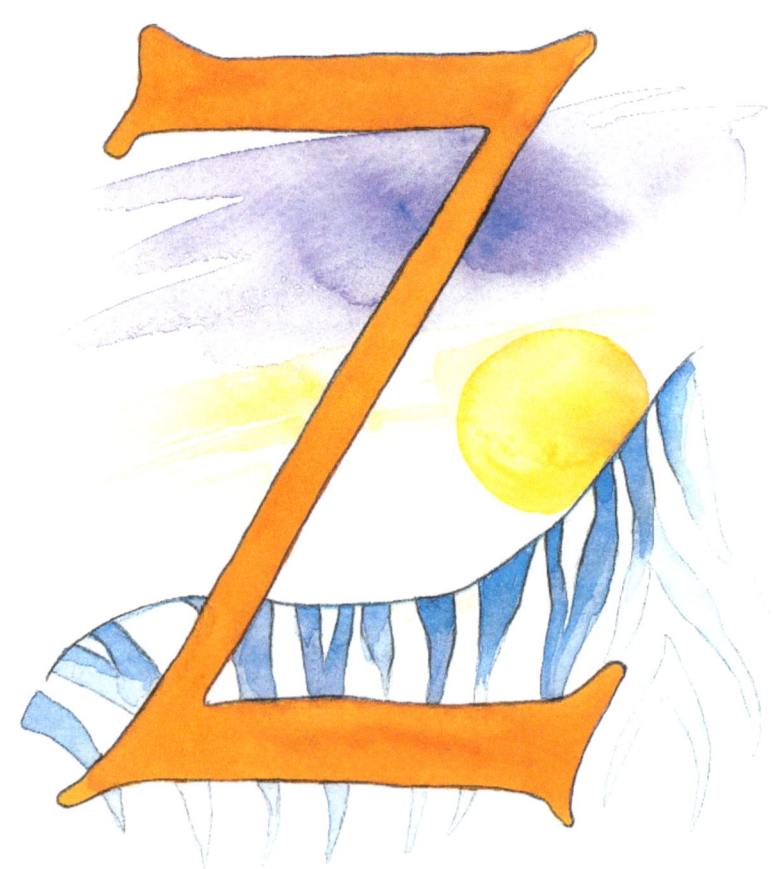

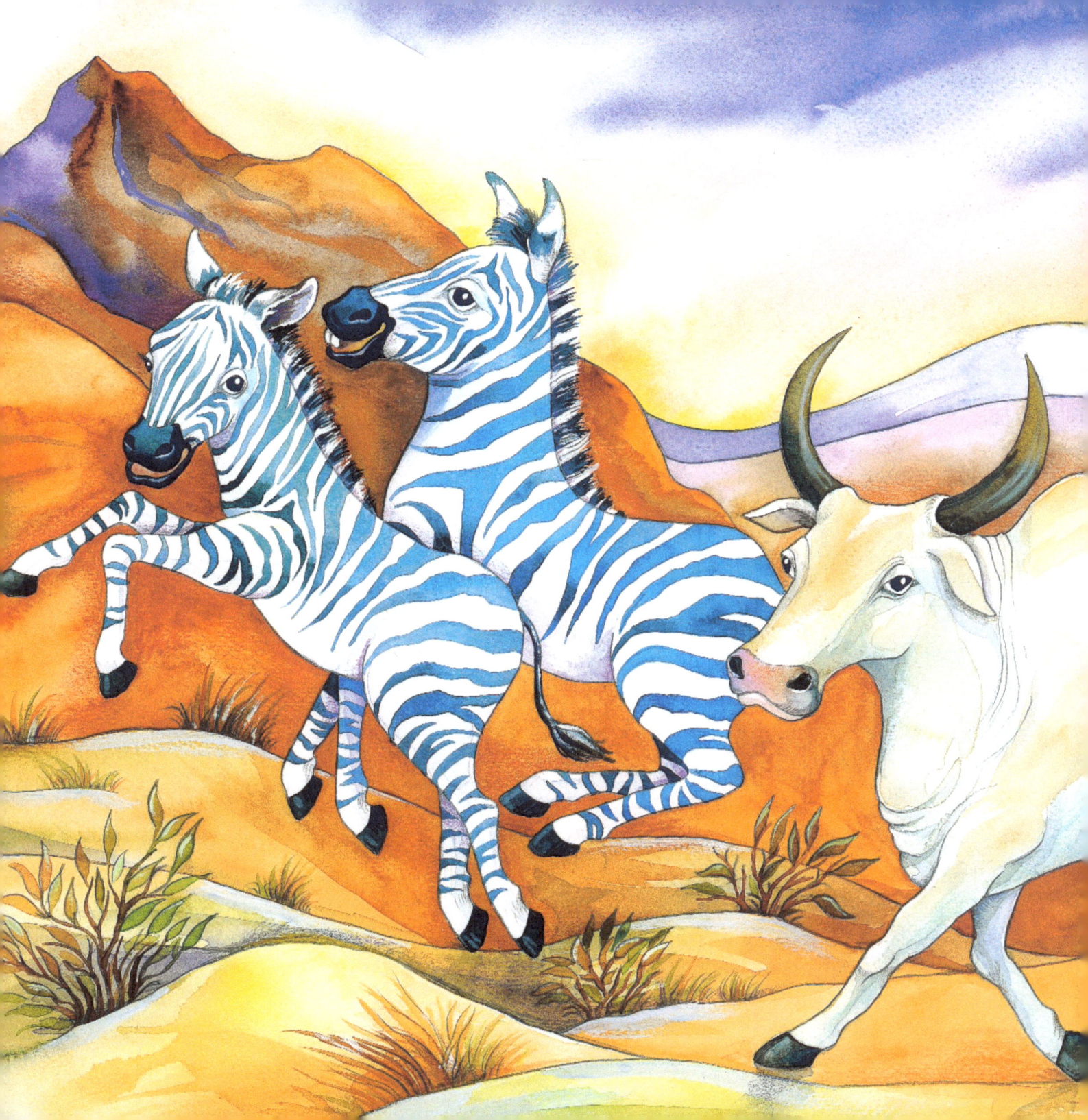

Glossary

acorn – the seed or fruit of an oak tree.

antlers – the branched horns of any animal of the deer family.

bamboo – a tall tree-like plant with many hard, hollow stems.

beak – the horny part of a bird's mouth; a bill.

beast – a wild animal.

below – under, beneath.

bison – the American buffalo with a large head and shaggy fore parts that grazes on the prairie.

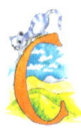

cactus – a desert plant with a thick trunk and sharp spikes.

chase – to run after someone in order to catch; to hunt.

chew – to grind, crush, or gnaw with the teeth.

clever – smart, intelligent; able to do things quickly and easily.

come across – to meet by chance.

desert – a dry region, largely treeless and sandy.

dinosaur – large reptile creatures that lived in prehistoric times.

discover – to find or find out about something.

dragon – a huge mythical fire-breathing monster.

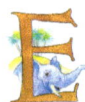

elephant – a large animal of Africa and Asia with tusks and a long trunk.

except – not including; leaving out.

extinct – no longer living; when the last member of a species dies, the species is extinct.

ex libris – Latin phrase meaning "from the library of."

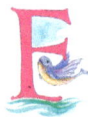

fangs – long, pointed, hollow teeth in snakes and spiders that pierce flesh and inject venom.

fate – what happens or has happened to a person or a thing; fortune.

feast – a large and fancy meal.

flamingo – a large pink bird with a long neck and legs.

footprint – a mark made by a foot.

fox – a wild animal of the dog family with thick fur and a long bushy tail.

G

gale – a very strong wind.

giraffe – an African animal with a long neck and legs and brown patches on its coat.

glow – to give off a steady light; shine.

graceful – elegant; having or showing grace.

grazing – eating growing grass or plants.

H

hare – an animal like a rabbit but larger with long and strong back legs.

heron – a large, long-legged bird that lives near wetlands.

hippo – hippopotamus; Greek for "river horse"; a large plant-eating mammal that lives in or near the rivers of Africa.

horn – a hard outgrowth on the heads of various hoofed animals.

huge – very large; immense; enormous.

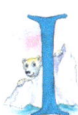

I

iceberg – a great mass of ice broken off from a glacier and floating in the sea.

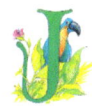

J

jagged – uneven and sharp.

jaguar – a large, spotted wildcat of tropical America, similar to a leopard.

jungle – land covered with thick growth of trees, tall vegetation and vines; a tropical forest.

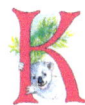

K

kangaroo – a jumping Australian animal; the female has a pouch in which she carries her young.

koala – a small bear-like Australian animal that lives in eucalyptus trees and feeds on their leaves.

L

lazily – moving slowly, in a relaxed manner.

lion – a large, powerful wild cat with a smooth, light-brown coat and a loud roar.

lounge – to stand, sit, or lie in a lazy and relaxed way.

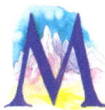

M

mountain – an area of land that rises high above its surroundings; a high, steep hill.

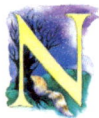

neck – the part of the body that joins the head to the shoulders.

night – the time between sunset and sunrise, especially the hours of darkness.

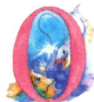

ocean – the great mass of salt water that covers almost three quarters of the earth's surface.

odd – not ordinary or usual; strange; peculiar.

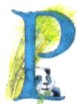

panda – a large bear-like black-and-white mammal native to bamboo forests in China and Tibet.

peacock – a male pheasant with brilliant tail feathers, which can be spread like a fan.

peek – to look at something secretly or quickly.

plain – a large, flat area of land without trees.

plume – a large, fluffy feather.

pointy – having a sharp end.

poison – a toxic substance causing illness or death when eaten, drunk, or absorbed even in small quantities.

polar bear – a large white bear that lives in the Arctic.

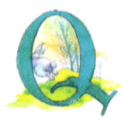

quick – rapid; swift; moving with speed.

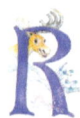

race – to run or move very fast.

raccoon – a furry North American night animal with a bushy tail and sharp snout.

reindeer – a deer with large branching antlers from Lapland.

roadrunner – a long-tailed, fast-running, cuckoo bird of the American Southwest.

roam – to wander aimlessly.

rough – stormy, severe, harsh.

rugged – having a rough, uneven surface.

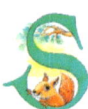

shaggy – rough; having long, untidy hair or fur.

squirrel – a small, bushy-tailed animal that lives in trees.

stash away – to hide or store away in a secret place.

steep – sloping at a sharp angle.

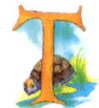

tale – story, legend.

tangle – to twist together in a confused mass.

tiger – a large, fierce animal of the cat family with a striped coat.

turtle – a sea animal with a soft body protected by a hard shell.

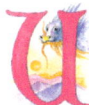

unicorn – an imaginary creature with a horse's body and a single twisted horn in the middle of its forehead.

undisturbed – not disturbed or bothered.

unseen – not seen, invisible.

untrue – not true, false.

unusual – not usual or ordinary; uncommon

vampire bat – a bat from South America that feeds on the blood of living animals.

venomous – capable of giving a poisonous bite or sting.

viper – a venomous snake with large fangs.

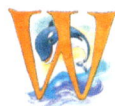

walrus – a large long-tusked sea animal of the Arctic Ocean.

whale – a large marine mammal related to dolphins.

wind up – end up in a certain way or place.

wrangle – take part in a noisy or angry quarrel.

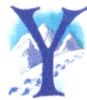

yeti – a large, hairy man-like creature said to live in the highest part of the Himalayas.

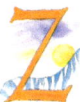

zebra – a horse-like wild animal of Africa with dark stripes.

zebu – an ox-like animal of Asia and Africa with a hump on its shoulders.

zoo – a park where wild animals are kept for display and study.

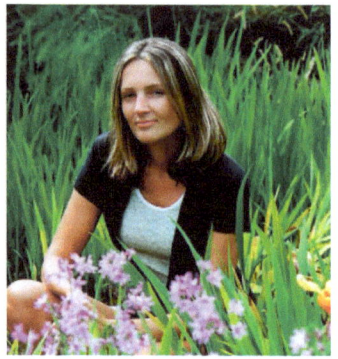

Triin in the Botanical Gardens of Tallinn, Estonia.

About the artist

Triin Tõugjas is from Tartu, Estonia. At the age of 10 she enrolled herself in the Art School for Children and began her studies in drawing, painting, sculpture, composition, and art history. She graduated from Tartu Art School, where she specialized in leather art. As a freelance artist, Triin pursues her interests in photography, textiles, and interior design. Since the publication of ABC Zoo, Triin has illustrated three other children's books published in Finland.

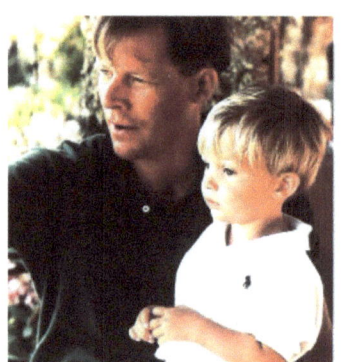

Studying flamingos in the Parrot Jungle of Miami, Florida.

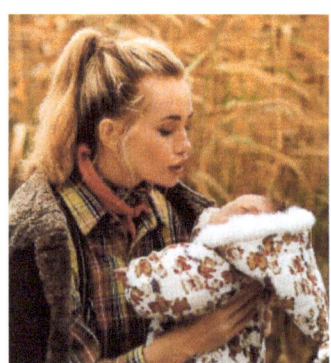

Helje in Stockholm's archipelago, Sweden.

About the authors

Christopher Bollyn is an independent journalist and author. Helje Kaskel is an English teacher and co-author of several English textbooks. The parents of two children, they believe that young readers deserve inspiring books with memorable illustrations to nurture early learning and curiosity.

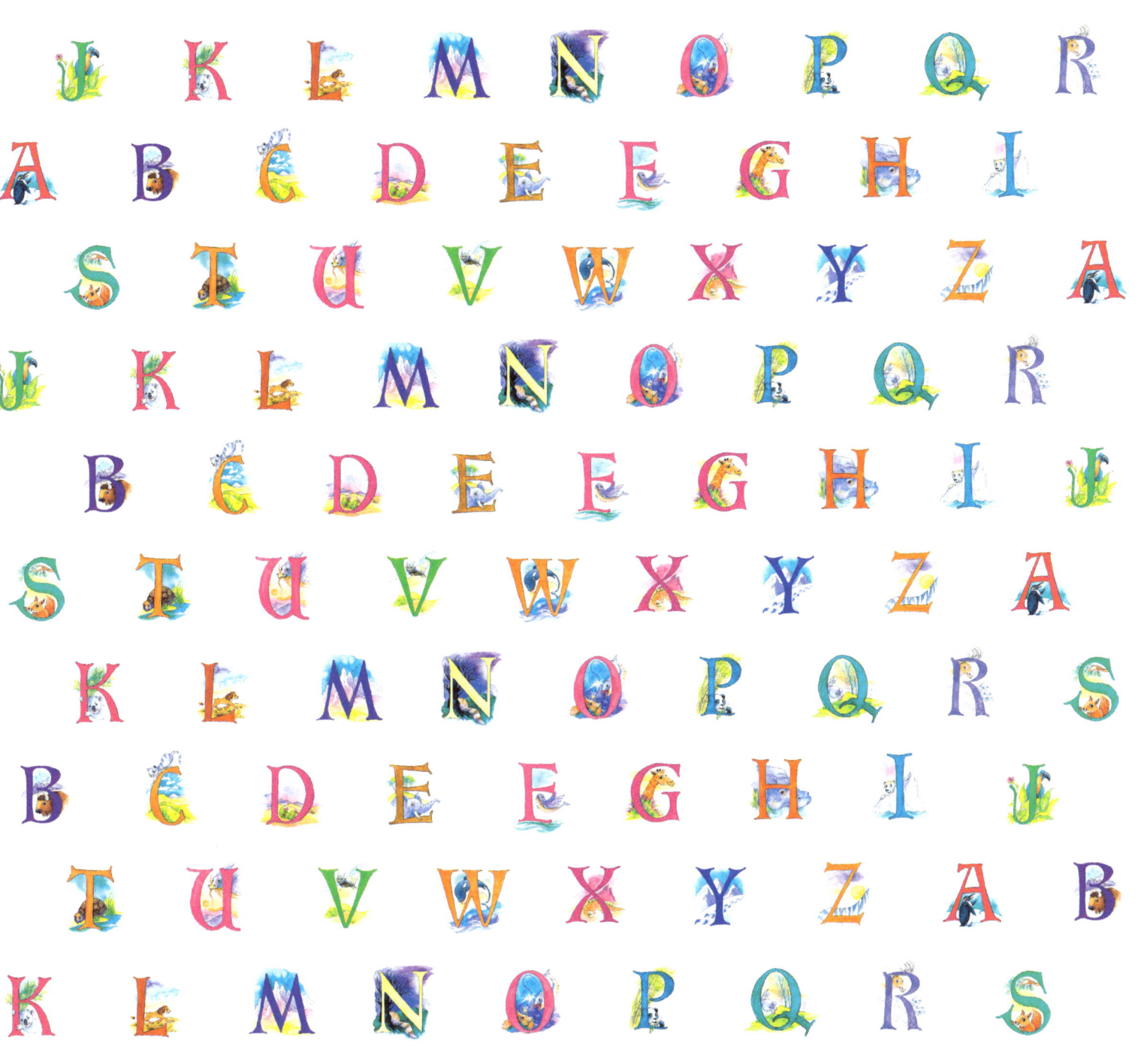

www.ingramcontent.com/pod-product-compliance
Lightning Source LLC
Chambersburg PA
CBHW050755180526
45159CB00003B/1465